M000251403

Pages
for iPad

NOLAN HESTER

 Peachpit Press

Visual QuickStart Guide
Pages for iPad
Nolan Hester

Peachpit Press
1249 Eighth Street
Berkeley, CA 94710
510/524-2178
510/524-2221 (fax)

Find us on the Web at www.peachpit.com
To report errors, please send a note to errata@peachpit.com
Peachpit Press is a division of Pearson Education

Associate Editor: Valerie Witte
Production Editor: David Van Ness
Compositor: David Van Ness
Developmental and Copy Editor: Kelly Kordes Anton
Proofreader: Patricia Pane
Indexer: Rebecca Plunkett
Interior Design: Peachpit Press
Cover Design: RHDG / Riezebos Holzbaur, Peachpit Press
Logo Design: MINE™ www.minesf.com
All example photographs: copyright ©2011 by Nolan Hester

ISBN-13: 978-0-321-75138-6
ISBN-10:   0-321-75138-8

9 8 7 6 5 4 3 2 1

Printed and bound in the United States of America

Dedication

To Mary, for being right there as we push ahead in this unknown adventure called life.

And everyone pushing the boundaries of where art and devices such as the iPad can take us.

Special Thanks to...

Valerie Witte, my editor, for her patience and skill in getting this one out the door,

David Van Ness for pulling all the pieces together in his usual sharp layouts,

Kelly Kordes Anton for a close editing that kept me on the right page,

Rebecca Plunkett for pitching in to generate the index under a tight deadline,

Tom Negrino and Chris Fehily, the authors of Peachpit's *Keynote for iPad: Visual QuickStart Guide* and *Numbers for iPad: Visual Quick-Start Guide*, respectively, for their camaraderie and fast answers,

Scott Cowlin for doing the unthinkable—loaning me his iPad for 10 long days—until mine arrived,

and all the other great folks at Peachpit who brought me on board the iPad book express.

Contents at a Glance

Table of Contents

Introduction

Up for an adventure? I hope so, because Pages for iPad—and the iPad it runs on—are so new it's mostly unknown territory ahead. There'll be some bushwhacking, no doubt. But there's also great fun ahead as you blaze the trail for those back at their offices and desks. Just be sure to bring along this book. It forms a perfect stack with the iPad—try it and see—and helps protect your screen wherever you're headed.

Using This Book

Like all of Peachpit's Visual QuickStart Guides, this book uses lots of screen shots to guide you through the entire process of creating Pages for iPad documents. Whether it's generating and styling text, crafting headlines, importing photos, adding charts and tables, and shuttling it all between the iPad and your main computer, we're with you at every step. Succinct captions explain all the major functions and options. Ideally, you should be able to quickly locate what you need by scanning the headlines and illustrations. Once you find a relevant topic, dig into the text for the details. Sidebars, which run in a light-beige box, highlight a particular topic, such as adding background images to your documents.

This book's companion website (www.waywest.net/pages4ipad) has example documents and images from the book that you can download to work through many of the tasks step by step. The site also features tips on how to get the most from Pages for iPad. Feel free to write me at books@waywest.net with your own tips—or any mistakes you may find.

1

Pages for iPad Overview

Many of us escaped our desks some time ago, thanks to laptops and netbooks. But the combination of the iPad and Pages for iPad offers even more flexibility. At 1.5 pounds, your iPad definitely can take the roads less traveled—and with Pages for iPad, you can publish the journal, photos, and maps of what you encounter along the way.

In This Chapter

Combo with a Difference

The iPad is such an integral part of using Pages for iPad that it can be tough to evaluate them separately. For example, at 132 pixels per inch, the iPad's screen is much sharper than many larger computer monitors. That makes for more than good-looking photos and charts in Pages for iPad. Text also is crisp, so the reality of spending hours in a small-screen Pages for iPad universe proves less daunting than it sounds.

Obviously, the iPad's small physical and computational footprint imposes genuine limits on Pages for iPad. Out of the box, for example, the iPad has no external keyboard. That might seem like a deal killer for anyone hoping to use Pages for iPad for long documents. Ditto when it comes to the screen keyboard's lack of a tab or arrow keys. But you can add a keyboard dock or wireless keyboard, both of which operate virtually identically as those on desktop Macs.

In using your iPad and Pages for iPad, you'll often find yourself juggling positives and negatives. A typical scenario: Toss the iPad in a bag, head out for the weekend, and slip in a bit of work on that Pages document. You can't necessarily do all the final formatting that you've come to expect on your main computer. So you sync iPad and computer when you get back to town and finish it there. You have to export a Pages for iPad document back to a regular computer to print anyway, so that's not as roundabout as it sounds. And it was nice to get out town—without toting a whole bag of computer gear.

Market
Outlook
Wet weather throughout the
spring cut both ways for
farmers. It kept temperatures
down, allowing better
ripening. But it also pushed
back to-market dates.

Wet weather throughout the
spring cut both ways for
farmers. It kept temperatures
down, allowing better ripening.
But it also pushed back to-market dates.

Wet weather throughout the spring cut both
ways for farmers. It kept temperatures down, allowing
better ripening. But it also pushed back to-market dates.
Wet weather throughout the spring cut both ways for
farmers. It kept temperatures down, allowing better
ripening. But it also pushed back to-market dates.

A Pages for iPad makes it easy to mix text, headlines, and images in creating your documents.

TABLE 1.1 Comparing Pages on the iPad and Mac

Pages Feature	iPad	Mac
Revision Tracking	No	Yes
Add Bookmarks	No	Yes
Read Bookmarks	No	Yes
Preserve Bookmarks	No	Yes
Add, Edit, Manage Citations (using EndNote X2)	No	Yes
Add Comments	No	Yes
View Comments	No	Yes
Create Hyperlinks	No	Yes
Convert Text to Table	No	Yes
Read Text-Converted Table	Yes	Yes
Restyle Text-Converted Table	No	Yes
Save Custom Text Styles	No	Yes
Create Custom Chart Styles	No	Yes
Word Count	No	Yes

Pages vs. Pages

Clearly, Pages for iPad offers fewer features and less control than its full-blown cousin. (See **Table 1.1**, "Comparing Pages on the iPad and Mac" at left.) Pages for Mac comes with 180 templates; the iPad comes with 15. Pages for Mac lets you link text boxes, Pages for iPad doesn't. The Mac version can do mail merges. The iPad can't. You get the idea.

But a feature-by-feature Pages smackdown risks missing the big picture of all you can do on a tiny iPad **A**. Instead of seeing Pages for iPad as some sort of poor cousin, think of it as a quick-response field unit able to go almost anywhere. Remember, this is Pages for iPad 1.1. It *will* evolve—as will the iPad itself with expected updates not far around the corner.

Text Options

For a true font hound, the 40-plus font families available on the iPad are lean pickings. But those that are available represent a nice mix of serif, sans-serif, script, and symbol fonts 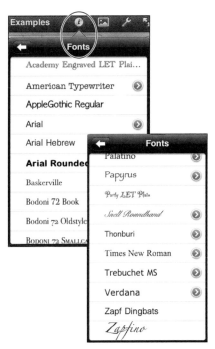. Certainly, more than enough options exist to get you going on a project. When you need more choices and control, you can export the iPad document to Pages for Mac.

You'll also find 12 paragraph styles, ranging from chapter titles to headings, body text, and labels ⓑ. You can customize each style ⓒ. Unfortunately, you cannot save your custom style settings as you can on Pages for Mac. (For more, see "Working with Text" on page 51.)

ⓐ Fonts A-Z: The 40 font families included with Pages for iPad provide plenty of choices.

ⓑ You can customize the 12 paragraph styles for a document, but you cannot save those changes for use with other documents.

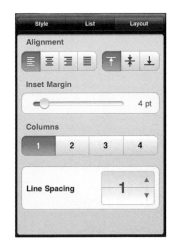

ⓒ You can fine-tune options such as alignment and line spacing for selected text using the Layout tab by tapping ⓘ.

A Strange but true: Your Mac uses iTunes to move iPhoto images onto your iPad.

B The Media tab gives you immediate access to all your iPad's photos, organized as albums.

Image Options

Pages for iPad offers direct access to all the photos you've imported into your iPad. Your Mac uses iTunes as the hub for syncing everything with your iPad. For that reason, you wind up using *iTunes* to pull in photos from your *iPhoto* albums **A**. It sounds odd, but the nice thing is your iPad organizes your images into photo albums with names mirroring those on your Mac. Just tap the [image] in the document toolbar and you'll find them in the Media tab **B**. It makes for easy navigation of all your iPad photos. Videos, also reached using the Media tab, can be added to documents as easily as photos **C**. (For more, see "Working with Images and Shapes" on page 73.)

C Videos, also accessed via the Media tab, can be added to documents as easily as photos.

Shape Options

The Shapes tab offers 15 basic shapes in six different color schemes 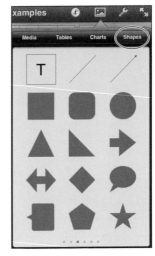. You can add shapes to documents as decorative elements or as text boxes. By scaling, stacking, and rotating the shapes, it's easy to quickly generate designs **B**. Used in combination with text, shapes can draw attention to labels and callouts **C**. To add one to a document, you simply tap the shape and drag it onto the page. (For more on this, see "Working with Images and Shapes" on page 73.)

A The Shapes tab offers 15 basic shapes in six different color schemes.

B By stacking multiple shapes—and changing the stacking order—you can generate a variety of decorative page elements.

C Used in combination with text, shapes can draw attention to labels and callouts.

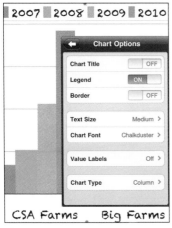

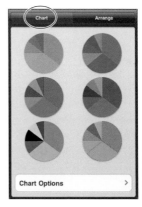

Chart Options

The Charts tab includes nine different types of charts , making it likely you'll find one to match your needs. After you insert a chart, there are plenty of options for customizing it, including the look of the title, legend, borders, and font **B**. One example of the clever touches you find throughout the iPad is the way you edit the data in charts. Double-tap the chart and it flips around to reveal the numbers **C**. While you don't have the myriad color choices found in Pages for Mac's charts, the iPad's charts offer pretty nice-looking preset color combinations **D**. (For more on this, see "Working with Charts" on page 101.)

A With nine different types of charts, you'll likely find one to match your needs.

B Chart Options include formatting choices for items such as title, legend, borders, text size, and font.

C Space-saving shortcut: Double-tapping a chart flips it around so that you can edit the data.

D You can't pick individual chart colors, but you can choose from preset combinations.

Table Options

Much like its approach to charts, Pages for iPad offers a limited but nice set of tables **A**. It's easy to customize the preset table styles by applying borders, alternating row patterns, grids, and headers **B**, **C**. While you cannot directly save your customized table formatting, you can duplicate the table, then use it again with new numbers. (For more on this, see "Working with Tables" on page 115.)

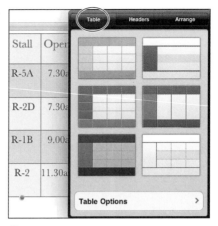

A Tables come in a variety of preset styles.

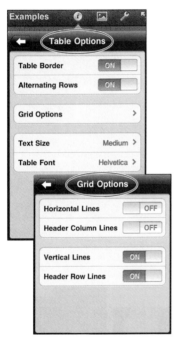

B It's easy to customize the preset table styles by applying borders and alternating row patterns and various grid styles.

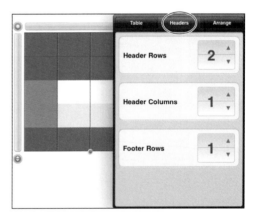

C You can add as many header columns and rows as you need, along with footer rows.

Working with Pages for iPad

If you're an old hand at using an iPad, you can skip to "Selecting Text" on page 19. If, however, you're learning how to use the iPad at the same time you're learning Pages for iPad, start here with the next section, "Moving Around the iPad."

In This Chapter

Moving Around the iPad

Aside from a dimpled button on the front and three low-profile buttons on the edges, you communicate with the iPad using its touch-sensitive screen. The iPad recognizes a number of "gestures," the most obvious of which is touching a screen icon to trigger an action. To save you some time, here's a rundown on the iPad's main gestures. Gestures specific to Pages for iPad are explained throughout the book as you need them.

To select or open items:

- Touch or "tap" a screen item to select or open it.

To scroll across or down the screen:

- Instead of using a mouse pointer to drag a scroll bar, drag your finger across or up and down the iPad screen.

To scroll across multiple screens:

- This is similar to a regular iPad scroll, but it's done by dragging your finger more quickly. Done vertically, it's called a "flick"; if you do this horizontally, then it's a "swipe." Examples include flicking down a Web page or swiping through document pages.

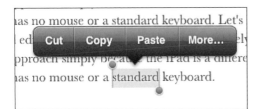

A Touch the screen and hold your finger there until a pop-up bar appears offering several choices.

Summer Bounty

Let's start by looking at how to select and edit text. Some things will seem

B Select an object by tapping it once, and it displays small square "handles" along the edges.

C Put one finger (or thumb) on the selected object, and pivot another finger around it. The selected object swings in the same direction.

To zoom in or out:

- Touch and spread two fingers on the screen to zoom in for a closer look. This "pinch" works great for seeing or selecting smaller screen items, such as tiny text.

- Touch and pull together two fingers on the screen to zoom out. This is sometimes called a "reverse pinch." Done in tandem with the pinch, it's easy to toggle between a far-out and in-close view of documents.

To trigger a contextual menu:

- If you touch the screen and hold your finger there for a moment, a pop-up bar appears offering several choices **A**. This is the iPad's equivalent to the right-click, or pop-up, contextual menus often used by keyboard-driven computers. Pages for iPad is packed with pop-up bars, as you'll see in the chapters ahead.

To rotate an object:

1. Select an object by tapping it once. The object displays small square "handles" along the edges **B**, similar to what you'd see if using a mouse pointer in Pages for Mac.

2. Now put one finger (or thumb) on the object and pivot another finger around it. The selected object swings in the same direction **C**. Practice this two or three times, and the gesture quickly feels natural.

TIP You can rotate photos in Pages for iPad but not charts or tables.

Using the Screen Keyboard

If you're not using an external keyboard, the iPad displays the screen keyboard only when it's needed. The screen keyboard automatically orients itself to the iPad's vertical (Portrait) or horizontal (Landscape) position. You can lock the screen in its current orientation by pressing the small screen-lock button found at the top-right edge (in Portrait mode).

To see the screen keyboard:

- If you haven't yet launched Pages, you can test the screen keyboard by swiping the main screen to the right. The iPad's search function appears . When Pages is running, the keyboard appears when you tap within any *editable* text area.

To hide the screen keyboard:

- Click the screen keyboard's bottom-right key (⌨), and it slides out of sight.

Ⓐ Swipe to the right across the main screen to display iPad's search area, where the screen keyboard appears automatically. This works only if no external keyboard is connected.

B The screen keyboard when it's switched to its numbers display.

C The screen keyboard when it's switched to its symbols display.

D If you press and hold the .com key, a pop-up bar lets you choose **.edu**, **.org**, or **.net**.

To switch among the screen keyboards:

- To switch from the default letters keyboard to the numbers-punctuation keyboard **B**, press the `.?123` key.

- To switch from the numbers-punctuation keyboard to the symbols keyboard **C**, press the `#+=` key.

- To switch from the symbols keyboard back to the numbers-punctuation keyboard, press the `123` key.

- To switch from the symbols keyboard back to the letters keyboard, press the `ABC` key.

TIP Whenever the screen keyboard appears, it automatically displays the letters keyboard, no matter which keyboard was last used.

TIP There's no way to switch directly from the letters keyboard to the symbols keyboard.

TIP Whenever you select a Web address field, the keyboard displays a .com key. If you press and hold the .com key, a pop-up bar lets you choose .edu, .org, or .net **D**.

Using an External Keyboard

At the moment, the iPad supports two external keyboard options: the one included in the Apple iPad keyboard dock or a wireless keyboard. Using the iPad's Camera Connection Kit, some users have had luck connecting USB keyboards, but the results have been unpredictable. When you use an external keyboard, the screen keyboard is not available.

To use the iPad keyboard dock:

■ Insert the iPad into the keyboard dock, and the external keyboard is immediately available for Pages for iPad.

To use a wireless keyboard:

1. Start by turning on your wireless keyboard. On the iPad's main screen, tap the Settings app .

2. Tap General in the left categories column and then Bluetooth in the right options column **B**.

3. Slide the Bluetooth switch to turn it on. After a moment, the keyboard appears in the Devices list, but it is not yet paired with the iPad **C**.

A To connect a wireless keyboard to the iPad, start by tapping the Settings icon.

B Within Settings, tap the General option (left) and then turn on Bluetooth.

C The first time you use it, your keyboard needs to be paired with the iPad. Tap Not Paired below the Bluetooth switch.

"Apple Wireless Keyboard" would like to pair with your iPad.

Enter the passkey "687393" on "Apple Wireless Keyboard", followed by the return or enter key.

Cancel

D Use your external keyboard to enter the passkey number and press Return/Enter.

General   Bluetooth

Bluetooth   ON

Devices

Apple Wireless Keyboard   Connected

Now Discoverable

E Once paired, the wireless keyboard is connected to the iPad. To exit Settings, press the iPad's Home button.

4. Tap Not Paired below the Bluetooth switch. A dialog displays a number, which you enter using the wireless keyboard **D**.

5. Press Return/Enter. The dialog closes, and the iPad and keyboard connect **E**. In the future, the keyboard's automatically paired with the iPad whenever the keyboard is on. If the keyboard is turned off, the iPad displays its screen keyboard when needed.

6. Exit the Settings by pressing the iPad's Home button.

TIP If your wireless keyboard is already paired with another device, such as your Mac, you must first "disconnect" it (to use Apple's term for cancelling a wireless pairing). Once you do that, you can pair it with the other device. Reverse the process to switch the keyboard back to the original device. Each device recognizes the previously paired keyboard, saving you the step of typing in another passkey.

Opening Pages
for iPad

After downloading it from the App Store, the Pages for iPad app icon appears on the main screen.

Pages

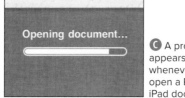 Ⓐ Tap once to open Pages for iPad.

To open Pages for iPad:

1. Tap the Pages for iPad icon once Ⓐ. The app opens and displays a single document called "Getting Started" Ⓑ.

2. Tap the document once to open it. A progress bar appears briefly as it opens Ⓒ.

My Documents (1 of 1)

Tap to Get Started with Pages.

Scroll through the document. Touch the images and text. And experience the most powerful word processor ever made for a mobile device.

Getting Started
Today, 3:41 PM

Ⓑ A single sample document called "Getting Started" appears once Pages for iPad opens.

Opening document...

Ⓒ A progress bar appears briefly whenever you open a Pages for iPad document.

A Summer in the West

It's a Wet Place

Lorem ipsum dolor sit amet
Ligula suspendisse nulla pretium, rhoncus tempor placerat fermentum, enim integer ad vestibulum volutpat. Nisl rhoncus turpis

Ⓐ Touch and hold your finger to trigger the appearance of the document navigator.

Ⓑ Lift your finger, and the document jumps to the chosen page.

Navigating in Pages for iPad

Pages for iPad includes two iPad-only tricks for navigating and viewing your documents. It also offers a handy way to hide or show the document toolbar.

To jump to any document page:

1. When viewing a multiple-page document, touch and hold anywhere along the screen's right edge. When the navigator appears, which looks like a magnifying glass, drag your finger up or down to scroll through the document Ⓐ. The page number also appears in the navigator.

2. Lift your finger off the screen when you see the page you want. The document jumps to that page Ⓑ.

To jump to top of document:

- To jump to the beginning of a multiple-page document, tap the black bar at the top of the screen (above the toolbar if it's on) . The document returns to the document's first page.

To hide or show document toolbar:

- To hide the document toolbar, tap the double arrow at the top right **D**. The toolbar disappears, giving you a full-screen view of your document **E**.

- To show the document toolbar, tap anywhere along the top edge of the document. The toolbar reappears.

C Jump to the beginning of a multiple-page document by tapping the narrow black bar across the top of the screen.

D Hide the document toolbar by tapping the double arrow at the top right.

E With the toolbar hidden, you can see the document without distraction. Tap anywhere across the screen's top to make the toolbar reappear.

A Double-tap a specific word to select it; the word is highlighted in blue with a pop-up bar above it.

B Triple-tap within a paragraph to select the entire paragraph.

C Tap some text, hold your finger for a moment, and a magnifying glass icon appears to help you to reposition the insertion point.

Selecting Text

Since it lacks a mouse pointer or regular keyboard, the iPad offers its own methods for selecting text and objects. If you're using a wireless keyboard or the iPad keyboard dock, the standard shortcuts of Cmd-X (cut), Cmd-C (copy), and Cmd-V (paste) are available as well. For now, we'll use the previously opened Getting Started document as our example.

To select text:

1. Do one of the following:

    Double-tap a specific word to select it. The word is highlighted in blue with a pop-up bar above it **A**.

    or

    Triple-tap a paragraph to select it. The entire paragraph is highlighted in blue with a pop-up bar above it **B**.

    or

    Tap some text and hold your finger there for a moment. A magnifying glass icon appears above your finger, allowing you to reposition the insertion point as necessary **C**. Lift your finger from the screen, and a pop-up bar appears above the insertion point.

2. Depending on your choice, select an option in the pop-up bar or use the screen or external keyboard to enter new text.

To expand or narrow a text selection:

■ After selecting a word or paragraph, tap either drag point (the blue buttons at each end) and drag to expand or narrow the selection 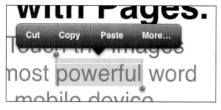.

TIP The drag points do not appear unless you select at least an entire word. After that, however, you can adjust the selection to include just part of a word.

To cut text:

1. Select the text you want to delete.

2. Tap Cut in the pop-up bar that appears **E** (top). The text is stored in the clipboard **E** (bottom).

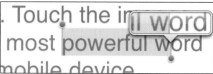

D Tap either drag point (the blue buttons) and drag it to expand or narrow the selection.

E Tap Cut in the pop-up bar, and the selected text is stored in the clipboard.

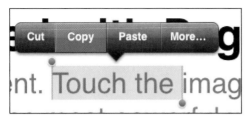

F Select the text you want to use and tap Copy in the pop-up bar.

G Position the insertion point and tap Paste in the pop-up bar. The previously copied text is inserted.

To copy and paste text:

1. Select the text you want to use.

2. When the pop-up bar appears, tap Copy **F**. The selection is copied to the iPad's clipboard.

3. Select some text you want to replace, or move to a new insertion point, and tap Paste in the pop-up bar **G** (top). The text copied in step 2 appears **G** (bottom).

TIP For more information on the pop-up bar's Copy Style, Replace, and Definition choices, see "To copy and paste a style" on page 55.

Putting It All Together

1. Use your finger to "swipe" from screen to screen and "flick" down a screen.

2. Use the "pinch" and "reverse pinch" to zoom in and out on a Web page.

3. Flick your way to the iPad's search area to test the screen keyboard.

4. Use the screen keyboard to switch among its three different versions.

5. If you have an external wireless keyboard, pair it with the iPad.

6. Open the Pages for iPad app and then the "Getting Started" document.

7. Use the double-tap and triple-tap to select words and paragraphs, respectively.

8. Tap and hold to use the magnifying glass to fine-tune a text selection.

9. Use the pop-up bar to cut, copy, and paste text.

Creating Documents

Creating documents with Pages for iPad is not that different from using a regular computer. What takes getting used to, however, is that you can't open up a folder and see all your documents or move them around. Instead, the iPad uses an entirely different approach to managing documents. And that means learning some new approaches to working with your documents in Pages for iPad.

Creating a New Document

When creating a new document, Pages for iPad offers you two choices. You can create a new blank document or you can create one based on a template. Pages for iPad includes 15 professionally designed templates for such items as formal letters and resumes, term papers and reports, and party invitations and flyers. With each template, you can substitute in your own text, headlines, and graphics. Or, use it as a starting point in creating your own custom design.

To create a blank document:

1. Launch Pages for iPad by tapping its app button **A**.

2. On the Pages for iPad's start screen, tap the New Documents button in the top left **B**.

3. Pages for iPad presents a grid of templates; tap Blank, the first one in the top row **C**.

4. Not surprisingly, a blank document appears. You could start entering text now, but first let's rename the document by tapping the top-left My Documents button **D**. (See the first Tip on page 27 for why this habit can help combat the forces of chaos and anarchy.)

A Launch the Pages for iPad by tapping its app button.

B On the start screen, tap the New Documents button at the top left.

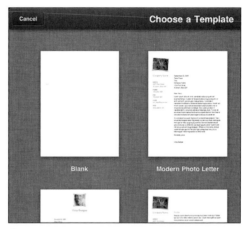

C In the grid of templates, tap Blank, the first one in the top row.

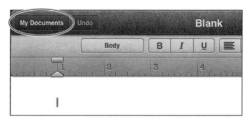

D To rename a document, tap the top-left My Documents button.

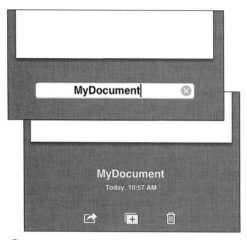

E In the My Documents view, your new document still bears the template's name, which can be confusing.

5. Tap the document's name to turn it into a text field, and type in your own name for the document **E**. To save the new name, tap Done on the screen keyboard or press Return/Enter on an external keyboard. The document displays its new name **F**. You now can add text, headers, or graphics in the document **G**. As always in Pages for iPad, the contents are saved automatically.

F Tap the name to make it a text field, type in a new name (top), and tap Done. The document now displays its new name (bottom).

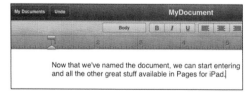

G After naming the document, you can add text, headers, or graphics to it.

To use a document template:

1. After launching Pages for iPad, tap the New Documents button at the top left of the My Documents view .

2. Flick through the grid of templates until you find one you prefer 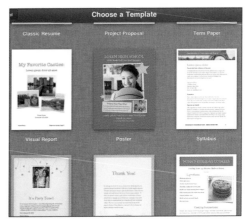. Tap that particular template to open it.

3. If the template meets your needs, tap the top-left My Documents button to rename it . (See first Tip.)

4. In the My Documents view, tap the new document's name and type in a new name 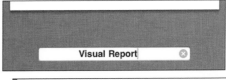. To save the new name, tap Done on the screen keyboard or press Return/Enter on an external keyboard.

H In the My Documents view, tap the top-left New Documents button.

I Look through the 15 professionally designed templates to find one you like.

J After choosing a template based on its general layout and purpose, tap the top-left My Documents button to give it a name of your own.

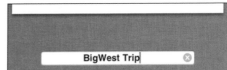

K In the My Documents view, tap the new document's name and type in a new name.

L When you tap a document, a progress bar appears while it opens.

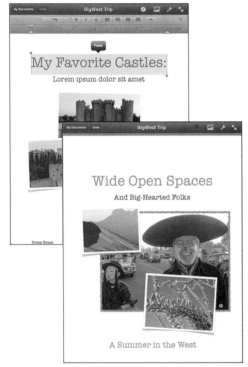

M Select items in your new template-based document to replace them with your own content.

N To replace photos in a new template-based document, tap the Image button.

5. Tap the renamed document to open it **L**.

6. Begin selecting and replacing the document's text blocks, headings, and graphics with content of your own **M**. The contents are saved automatically. (See second and third Tip.)

TIP In step 3, every time you open a template for a quick peek at its layout, Pages for iPad automatically saves it as a new document—using the same name as the template. This quickly gets confusing as the My Documents view becomes littered with these newly generated documents. To nip it in the bud, immediately rename the documents you intend to use and delete the accidental ones. (See "Deleting a Document" on page 29.)

TIP In step 6, you cannot select single placeholder words in a new template-based document. Instead, the entire text block is selected on the assumption that you'll replace all of it with your own text. Once you enter your own text, you can edit individual words or characters.

TIP In step 6, to replace photos in a new template-based document, but maintain their layout, tap the Image button in the bottom-right corner of a photo **N**. That takes you to the Photo Albums window where you can choose one of your own photos. (See "Inserting Images and Video" on page 76.)

Duplicating a Document

Just as you use Pages for iPad templates to get a jump-start on creating pages, you can duplicate your own pages to reuse them.

To duplicate a document:

1. If you're not already in the My Documents view, tap the top-left My Documents button.

2. Flick through your documents to find the one you want to duplicate. Tap the + button at the bottom of the screen and choose Duplicate Document from the popover **A**. The duplicate appears with "copy" added to the original name **B**.

3. You can leave the name unchanged, but to prevent confusion, you may want to rename it. To change it, tap the duplicate's name and type in a new name **C**. To save the new name, tap Done on the screen keyboard or press Return/Enter on an external keyboard. (See Tip.)

TIP In step 3, if you intend to use the duplicate as a template itself, give it a name that makes that obvious **C**.

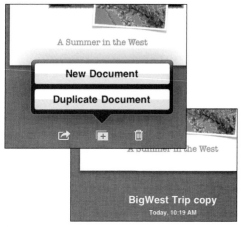

A Tap the + button at the bottom of the screen and choose Duplicate Document from the popover.

B The duplicate appears with "copy" added to the original name.

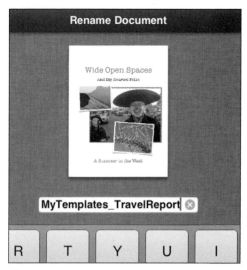

C If you rename the duplicate, use a name that makes its purpose obvious.

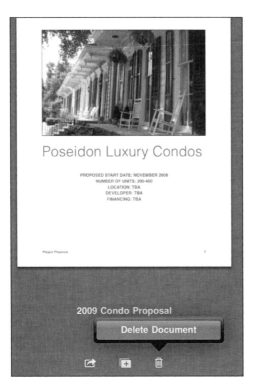

Deleting a Document

The iPad does not have a traditional set of folders in which to store and organize your Pages documents. That means it's more likely you'll need to occasionally delete unused or out-of-date documents to reduce clutter in the My Documents view.

To delete a document:

1. If you're not already in the My Documents view, tap the top-left My Documents button.

2. Flick through your documents to find the one you want to delete. Tap the Trash button at the bottom of the screen and choose Delete Document from the popover **A**.

Setting Page Margins and Size

In keeping with its graphics-based interface, Pages for iPad does away with number fields for setting page margins. Instead, it's a tap-and-drag affair. Similarly, choosing a page size involves tapping buttons.

By the way, setting page breaks and columns are covered in Chapter 5 since that's usually done as you add text to a page. Here, the focus is on setting up the overall document.

To set page margins:

1. Open the document and tap the 🔧 in the toolbar, and then tap Document Setup in the popover Ⓐ.

2. In the Document Setup view, touch and hold any arrow around the edge of the page Ⓑ. As you drag the arrow, the current margin width is displayed nearby. When the number shows the desired margin width, lift your finger to set the margin Ⓒ.

3. Adjust the other margins as needed.

4. When you're ready, tap Done in the toolbar's upper-left to close the Document Setup view Ⓓ.

TIP You'll need to turn the iPad to its vertical Portrait mode to look at the full-page view of any document.

Ⓐ To set the page margins, tap the 🔧 and then tap Document Setup in the popover.

Ⓑ In the Document Setup view, you can see the margins, header and footer placement, and page size at a glance.

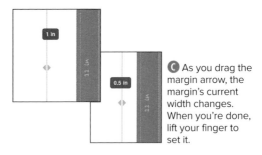

Ⓒ As you drag the margin arrow, the margin's current width changes. When you're done, lift your finger to set it.

Ⓓ Tap Done in the toolbar to close the Document Setup view.

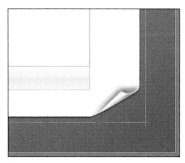

E To set the page size, tap the bottom-right corner of the page in the Document Setup view.

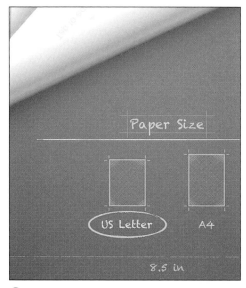

F Tap the paper size you want to use for the document, then tap the bottom-right corner to close the document.

To set page size:

1. To reach the Document Setup view, tap the 🔧 in the toolbar and then tap Document Setup in the popover.

2. Tap the curled paper edge at the bottom-right corner of the page **E**.

3. Beneath the virtual top sheet of paper, tap the paper size you want to use for the document **F**. The selected dimensions appear along the bottom and right edge.

4. After making your choice, tap the bottom-right corner again. The top sheet curls back into place. Tap Done in the toolbar to close the Document Setup view.

TIP You'll need to turn the iPad to its vertical Portrait mode to look at the full-page view of any document.

Adding Content to Headers or Footers

Every Pages for iPad template includes hidden formatting for headers and footers. They don't appear in your documents until after you add content to them within the Document Setup view. Besides adding text, you can insert one of several auto page-numbering styles. The same header and footer content is applied to every page in the document.

To add content to a header or footer:

1. Open the Document Setup view by tapping the ✐ in document toolbar. Tap Document Setup in the popover that appears **Ⓐ**.

2. Tap the header or footer to edit it **Ⓑ**. Three boxes appear in the header or footer with each representing a different alignment—flush left, centered, or flush right—for whatever text you enter **Ⓒ**. (See first Tip.)

Ⓐ To add content to a header or footer, tap the ✐ in the document's toolbar, and then tap Document Setup.

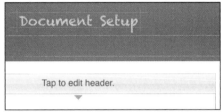

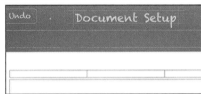

Ⓑ Tap the header or footer to enter content using one of three alignments.

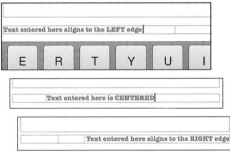

Ⓒ Tap one of the three boxes to enter text set flush left, centered, or flush right.

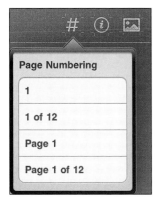

Page Numbering

1
1 of 12
Page 1
Page 1 of 12

D After choosing an alignment, you also can tap the # button to choose a page-number style from the popover.

Summer in the West

Page 1 of 2

E After closing the Document Setup view, the new content appears in the page's header or footer.

3. Do one of the following:

Type text into one of the alignment boxes for the header or footer **C**.

or

Tap an alignment box, then tap the # button in the document toolbar, and choose a page-number style in the popover **D**.

4. Tap Done to close the Document Setup view and your new header or footer content appears on the page **E**.

TIP It's easy to mistake the alignment choices in the header and footer for a three-cell table. However, you can only enter text in one "cell," not all three.

TIP To change the header and footer, double-tap it in the regular document view. The Document Setup view appears, enabling you to edit it directly.

Putting It All Together

1. Create a new blank document and close it.

2. Rename that document.

3. Reopen the document, add some text, and close it once more.

4. Create a new document based on one of the Pages for iPad templates.

5. Replace some of the text or photos in the new template-based document.

6. Make a duplicate of either document.

7. Now delete that duplicate.

8. Reopen your template-based document and change the page margins.

9. Add some text to that document's header and insert one of the auto page-numbering styles to the footer.

Importing and Exporting Documents

There are three ways to get documents in and out of Pages for iPad. You can use iTunes to shift files from your iPad to your Mac over the included USB cable. You also can email the documents. Or, you can share them with other iWork users logged into the iWork.com public beta. How best to pass documents back and forth from your iPad remains in flux, so check this book's companion site for updates: **www.waywest.net/pages4ipad/**.

Moving Files Using iTunes

Just as iTunes is your main method for syncing your iPad and computer, it's also the primary way to move documents between the two. The first time through, the steps seem needlessly complicated. After that, however, it makes sense and quickly becomes second nature.

To export from the iPad to your computer:

1. Swipe through your documents in the My Documents view until the one you want to export is centered on the screen. Tap the arrow button below the document and choose Export in the popover **A**.

2. In the Export Document dialog, tap one of the three available formats: Pages, PDF, or Word **B**. A progress bar tracks the export **C**.

3. Connect the iPad to your computer and open iTunes. Select your iPad when it appears in iTune's left column **D**.

A Tap the arrow button below the document and choose Export.

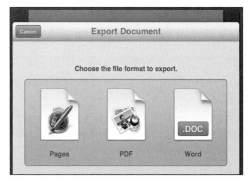

B Choose one of the three available formats in the Export Document dialog.

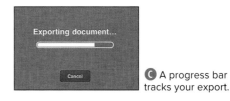

C A progress bar tracks your export.

D After connecting to your computer, select your iPad in the left column of iTunes.

File Sharing

The applications listed below can transfer

Apps

- DocsToGo
- GoodReader
- Keynote
- Numbers
- Pages

E Click the Apps tab, scroll down to the File Sharing section, and click Pages in the left column.

4. Click the Apps tab, scroll down to the File Sharing section, and click Pages in the left column **E**.

5. The right column lists all the Pages-created documents on your iPad. Select one and click the Save To button **F**. Navigate to the folder on your Mac where you want to copy the document and click Open **G**. The document is exported to that folder.

6. Open the Pages for Mac program, choose File > Open from the Menu bar, and navigate to the exported document to open it **H**.

TIP In step 3, it's fine if your iPad and Mac are already connected; just open iTunes.

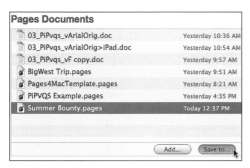

Pages Documents

03_PiPvqs_vArialOrig.doc	Yesterday 10:36 AM
03_PiPvqs_vArialOrig>iPad.doc	Yesterday 10:54 AM
03_PiPvqs_vF copy.doc	Yesterday 9:57 AM
BigWest Trip.pages	Yesterday 9:51 AM
Pages4MacTemplate.pages	Yesterday 8:21 AM
PiPVQS Example.pages	Yesterday 4:35 PM
Summer Bounty.pages	Today 12:37 PM

Add...   Save to...

F Select a document in the Pages Documents list and click Save To.

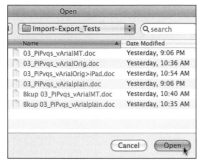

Open

Import-Export_Tests   Q search

Name	Date Modified
03_PiPvqs_vArialMT.doc	Yesterday, 9:06 PM
03_PiPvqs_vArialOrig.doc	Yesterday, 10:36 AM
03_PiPvqs_vArialOrig>iPad.doc	Yesterday, 10:54 AM
03_PiPvqs_vArialplain.doc	Yesterday, 9:06 PM
Bkup 03_PiPvqs_vArialMT.doc	Yesterday, 10:40 AM
Bkup 03_PiPvqs_vArialplain.doc	Yesterday, 10:35 AM

Cancel   Open

G Navigate to the folder on your Mac where you want to copy the document and click Open.

H The exported document opened in Pages for Mac.

To import from your computer to the iPad:

1. Connect the iPad to your computer and open iTunes. Select your iPad when it appears in the left column of iTunes.

2. Click the Apps tab, scroll down to the File Sharing section, and click Pages in the left column.

3. Click Add at the bottom of the right column, which lists all the Pages-created documents already on your iPad 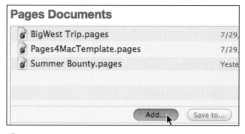.

4. On your computer, navigate to the document you want to import to the iPad and click Open . Your choice is added to the list of documents on the iPad .

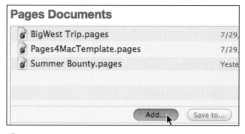

I Click Add at the bottom of the right column, which lists all the Pages-created documents already on your iPad.

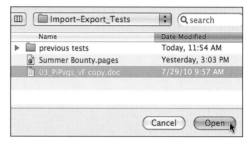

J Navigate to the document you want to import to the iPad and click Open.

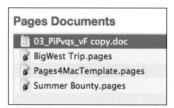

K Your choice is added to the list of documents on the iPad.

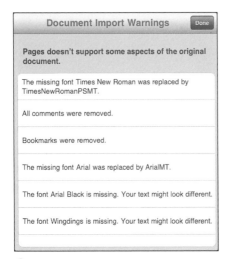

L In Pages for iPad, switch to the My Documents view and tap the folder button at the toolbar's far right.

M In the Import Document dialog, tap the document you added in step 4.

N The Document Import Warnings dialog lists any changes made during the import. Review the list and tap Done.

5. On your iPad, switch Pages to the My Documents view and tap the folder button at the far right of the toolbar L.

6. In the Import Document dialog, tap the document you added in step 4 M. A progress bar tracks the import and, most likely, a Document Import Warnings dialog lists any changes made during the import N.

Continues on next page

7. Review the list of changes, and tap Done. When the imported document opens, take a look to see what was lost in the translation. In many cases, the changes are minor 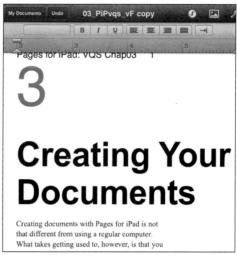. (For more information on dealing with format translation issues, especially Microsoft Word documents, see "Plays Well with Others?" on page 41.)

TIP Though you have to connect your iPad to your computer to import documents, you do not need to click the iTunes Sync button. Clicking the Add button in step 4 is all you need to do for the document to appear on your iPad.

TIP If there's a Pages for Mac template you like, you can import it into Pages for iPad. The transfer may change some fonts, but most of the layout comes through fine. It's an easy way to expand your Pages for iPad layout choices.

My Documents Undo 03_PiPvqs_vF copy

Pages for iPad: VQS Chap03   1

3

Creating Your Documents

Creating documents with Pages for iPad is not that different from using a regular computer. What takes getting used to, however, is that you

O For many imports, such as this Microsoft Word document, the formatting changes are minor.

Plays Well with Others?

When it comes to shuttling Pages and Microsoft Word documents between the iPad and a Mac, perfect back-and-forth translation has not yet arrived. But perfect's not necessary for a lot of word processing, and Pages for iPad does introduce new options for working beyond the office desk. As Pages for iPad is updated, surely some of the bumps will be smoothed out—at least between it and Pages for Mac. In the meantime, you can sidestep some problems by knowing where the translation process stumbles.

Fonts: With support for more than 40 fonts and font families, the iPad does a decent substitution job when it encounters a document using unavailable fonts. But it's not letter perfect. For example, the iPad supports Arial, perhaps the most common font family on the planet. But as you can see with items 4 and 5 in N on page 39, there are wrinkles for individual fonts, such as ArialMT and Arial Black. Symbol fonts, such as the commonly used Wingdings, get swapped out as well A.

Revisions, Comments, Bookmarks: Pages for iPad cannot read the revision-tracking features used by Pages for Mac and Microsoft Word. As a result, revisions are stripped out in the iPad version of the document. The same goes for the comments/annotation and bookmarking features. The revisions workaround is simple but cumbersome: use a unique name for each version of a document and keep the past versions on hand. Comments are tougher precisely because they're essential for collaboration on complicated documents. Word's revision, comments, and bookmarks are preserved by the strong-selling app Documents To Go, from Data-Viz. Hopefully, that puts extra pressure on Pages for iPad to work out these kinks quickly.

General Gremlins: You have to keep an eye out for the unexpected. For example, a Word document moved from the iPad back to a Mac might look nearly identical in Word's Normal view but not in the Page Layout view B, C.

03_PiPvqs_vF copy

Pages for iPad: VQS Chap03   10
[[PiPChap03_029_E.tif]]

E After closing the Document Setup view, the new content appears in the page's header or footer.

Tips

☐☐It's easy to mistake the alignment choices in the header and footer for a three-cell table. However, you can enter text in only one "cell," not all three.

A When the iPad can't find a similar font, it uses Helvetica, as it did here for the Wingdings character used as a bullet.

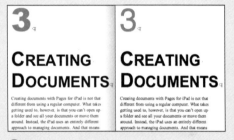

B Left: Microsoft Word document on a Mac. Right: Same document exported from an iPad back to the Mac. The "3" changed, but the document looks pretty good in Word's *Normal* view.

C Back on the Mac in Word's *Page Layout* view, you can see how the version exported from the iPad (right) forced the "3" to the right.

Moving Files Using Email

If you've set up your iPad for email, it's easy to email Pages and Microsoft Word documents as attachments. (To set up your iPad's email accounts, tap the Home screen's Settings > Mail, Contacts, Calendars > Mail, and at the same level, Accounts > Add Account.)

To email files from the iPad:

1. Swipe through the My Documents view until the document you want to email is centered on the screen. Tap the arrow button below the document and choose Send via Mail in the popover **A**.

2. In the Send via Mail dialog, tap one of the three available formats: Pages, PDF, or Word **B**. A "creating document" message appears briefly at the top of the dialog.

3. Type an address in the To: field, type in a message, and replace the Subject line if you don't want to use the default (the name of the attachment) **C**.

4. Tap Send at the top right. The email closes and you return to the My Documents view of your document. Depending on the size of the attachment, it may take several moments before you hear a sound like a plane taking off—the iPad's default mail-sent sound.

5. On your computer, use your email program to read the message, and open the document in Pages for Mac, Microsoft Word, or a PDF program, such as Preview or Acrobat.

A With the document you want to email centered in the My Documents view, tap the arrow button and choose Send via Mail.

B In the Send via Mail dialog, tap one of the three available export formats.

C The document appears as an email attachment. Add an address and message, then tap Send.

D Open the email containing the attachment, tap it, and choose Open in "Pages."

E Pages for iPad displays the emailed document.

F To leave the attachment's Quick Look view, choose Done or choose from the list in the Open In popover.

To import documents emailed to your iPad:

1. In the iPad's Mail program, open the email containing the attachment. Tap and hold your finger on the attachment and choose Open in "Pages" in the popover D. (See Tip.)

2. Pages for iPad opens and displays a progress bar during the import.

3. A Document Import Warnings dialog lists any changes made during the import. Review the list and tap Done. Pages for iPad displays the emailed document E.

TIP If you tap the attachment in step 1 without keeping your finger on the screen, it opens in Quick Look, which skips a lot of the formatting and lets you just check the contents. To leave the attachment's Quick Look view, tap the screen and choose Done or Open In from the slide-down toolbar F. Done returns you to the email; Open In displays a popover list of all your apps that can open the document.

Sharing Files Using iWork.com

Apple's online sharing service, iWork.com, has a few kinks to work out. Using iWork.com and a Web browser, you can add comments and notes to a Pages document. Currently, however, there is no way to actually view those comments on the iPad. Here's hoping this changes in the future. For more on using iWork.com, see **www.apple.com/support/iworkcom/**.

To send a document to iWork.com:

1. Swipe through your documents in the My Documents view until the one you want to use is centered on the screen. Tap the arrow button below the document and choose Share via iWork.com in the popover Ⓐ.

2. After a moment, the document is attached to a new email message. Type an address in the To: field, type in a message, and replace the Subject line if you don't want to use the default (the name of the attachment) Ⓑ.

Ⓐ Tap the arrow button below the selected document and choose Share via iWork.com.

Ⓑ Add an address and message to the email containing the document and tap Share.

C Tap the Sharing Options button to change the attachment's name, require would-be viewers to enter a password, or allow comments.

D Once the upload is done, Pages asks if you want to view it in your browser. If not, tap OK to stay in Pages.

3. Tap the Sharing Options button if you want to change the attachment's name, require would-be viewers to enter a password, or allow comments C. By default, all three formats—Pages, PDF, and Word—can be uploaded. Use the slider buttons to turn off any format.

4. Tap outside the Sharing Options dialog to close it. Then tap Share to upload the document and to send the message to your colleagues. In the My Documents view, a progress bar tracks the preparation and copying of the file to iWork.com.

5. Once the upload is done, Pages asks if you want to view the document at iWork.com by automatically launching your browser D. If not, tap OK to close the dialog and stay in the My Documents view.

To download a document from iWork.com:

1. Use your iPod's Mail app to open the message inviting you to view a shared document at iWork.com 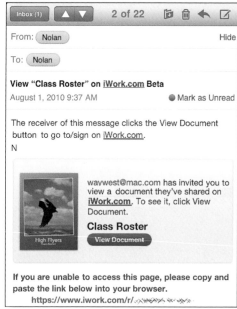. (See the first Tip.)

2. Tap the View Document button and tap Open . (See the second Tip.)

E Open the message inviting you to view a shared document at iWork.com.

F Tap the View Document button and choose Open.

G Sign in with your Apple ID when your browser takes you to iWork.com.

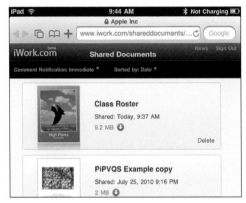

H Your iWork.com home page lists all the documents being shared.

3. Sign in when your browser takes you to iWork.com G.

4. Your iWork.com home page lists all the documents being shared with you H. Find the document you need and tap the blue arrow (click if you're using a regular computer) to download it.

5. Once the Web download finishes, the document opens in Pages.

TIP Sharing work across machines is the whole point of iWork.com. You do not need an iPad (or a Mac) to view the document—just a Web browser and iWork login, which uses your existing Apple iTunes or MobileMe ID.

TIP If your browser is set to block images, the View Document button won't appear, so tap/click the link at the bottom of message.

Printing iPad Documents

There's currently no way to connect a printer directly to your iPad. Instead, you need to export iPad documents to a computer and print them there.

To print documents:

1. Use any of the three methods explained earlier to export your document to a connected computer.

2. On the computer, open the document in Pages for Mac, Microsoft Word, or a PDF program, such as Preview or Acrobat.

3. Print the document as you normally would.

Putting It All Together

1. Select a Pages document in the My Documents view and export it.

2. Connect your iPad to your computer and use iTunes to save the exported file to a folder on the computer.

3. Use iTunes to move a document from your computer to your iPad.

4. Select a Pages document in the My Documents view and email three different versions to yourself: one in Pages, one in PDF, and one in Microsoft Word's .doc format.

5. Use your iPad's Mail app to open those same three emails and import the different formats into Pages.

6. Use Pages to send a document to yourself or a friend at iWork.com.

7. Use your Apple ID (create one first if necessary), to log in to iWork.com and open the document you sent.

8. Use iWork.com to add a few notes and comments to the shared document.

9. Use iTunes, email, or iWork.com to move a document from your iPad to your computer, and then print it as usual.

5

Working with Text

Pages for iPad may not yet equal its larger cousin, Pages for Mac, but it offers very robust text-handling features. As you'd expect, it excels at styling text. What you might not expect is how well it handles the ins and outs of lists, tab stops, and the creation and adjustment of multiple text columns.

In This Chapter

Styling Text and Paragraphs

Pages for iPad's document toolbar and ruler sit right above documents as you work with them. Together, they put the most commonly used text functions just a tap or two away. It's easy to quickly apply such mainstays as boldface or italic. But there's also a great way to copy all the styling details applied to one paragraph and "paste" them to another paragraph.

To show or hide the document toolbar:

- If the document toolbar is hidden, tap anywhere along the screen's top edge **Ⓐ**. The toolbar drops into view **Ⓑ**.
- To hide the document toolbar, tap ⌧ at its right end **Ⓑ**. The toolbar slides out of view **Ⓐ**.

TIP The document toolbar appears automatically whenever you select text or an object in a document.

To show or hide the ruler:

- Make sure the document toolbar is visible, then tap anywhere along its bottom edge where the ruler is just visible **Ⓑ**. The ruler drops into view **Ⓒ**.
- To hide the ruler, tap ⓧ at its right end **Ⓒ**. The ruler tucks mostly out of sight under the toolbar **Ⓑ**.

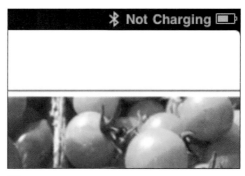

Ⓐ To show the document toolbar, tap anywhere along the screen's top edge.

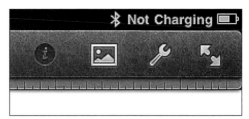

Ⓑ To hide the document toolbar, tap the ⌧.

Ⓒ To hide the ruler, tap the ⓧ.

D Select the words or characters you want to change and tap one of the three buttons in the toolbar.

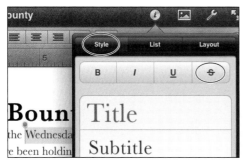

E In the popover's Style tab, tap ꜱ.

To apply bold, italic, or underline to text:

1. Select the words or characters you want to change. The document toolbar appears **D**.

2. Tap one of the three style buttons in the document toolbar A. The change is applied to the selected text.

TIP To undo a change, tap the relevant button a second time. If the text is not selected, reselect it first.

TIP Not every font family includes a bold or italic.

To apply strikethrough to text:

1. Select the words or characters you want to mark with strikethrough. The document toolbar appears.

2. Tap **ⓘ** in the toolbar, tap Style in the popover, and then tap ꜱ **E**.

3. The text is marked with a strikethrough. Tap anywhere on the screen to close the popover.

TIP To remove a strikethrough, select the text and repeat steps 2–3.

To change a paragraph's style:

Triple-tap a paragraph to select it, then do one of the following:

- Tap the ruler's paragraph-style button and flick down the popover to choose another style 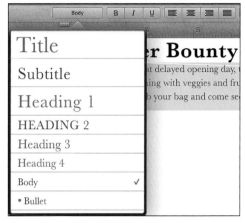. Tap the new style to apply it to the paragraph 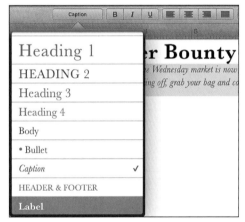.

  or

- Tap ⓘ in the toolbar, tap Style in the popover, flick down to another style, and tap it 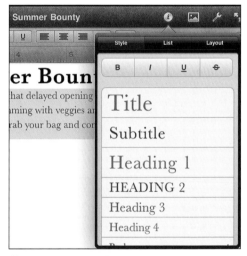. The new style is applied to the paragraph.

TIP To remove styling from selected text, tap the relevant button a second time. If the text is not selected, reselect it first.

F After selecting a paragraph, tap the ruler's paragraph-style button and flick down the popover to choose another style.

G Tap the new style to apply it to the paragraph.

H You also can tap ⓘ in the toolbar, tap Style in the popover, and flick down to another style.

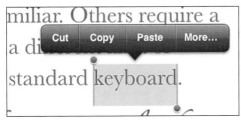

I Select the text whose style you want to *copy* and tap More.

J When the pop-up bar choices change, tap Copy Style.

K Select the text whose style you want to *change* and tap More.

L When the pop-up bar choices change, tap Paste Style.

To copy and paste a style:

1. Select the text whose style you want to *copy* and tap More in the pop-up bar **I**.

2. When the pop-up bar choices change, tap Copy Style **J**.

3. Select the text whose style you want to *change* and tap More in the pop-up bar **K**.

4. When the pop-up bar choices change, tap Paste Style **L**. The text's style changes **M**.

TIP Unlike Pages for Mac, you cannot create and save a new style for later use in Pages for iPad.

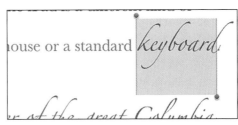

M The text's style changes.

Changing Text Colors and Fonts

Changing the text's font family is only slightly more involved than changing a typeface to bold or italic.

To change text size:

1. Select the text whose size you want to change and Tap **ⓘ** in the toolbar.

2. Tap Style in the popover, and scroll to the bottom to tap Text Options **Ⓐ**.

3. Tap the Text Options panel's up or down arrows to change the size of the text **Ⓑ**. The selected text changes size accordingly **Ⓒ**.

4. If you want to change another text option, tap the Color or Font sections. If the size is the only thing you want to change, tap anywhere outside the popover to return to your document.

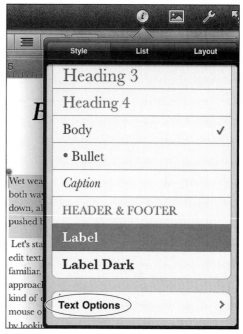

Ⓐ To reach the Text Options panel, tap **ⓘ** in the toolbar and tap Style in the popover. Scroll to the bottom and tap Text Options.

Ⓑ Tap the up and down arrows to change the selected text's size.

Ⓒ The selected text changes size based on which arrow you tap.

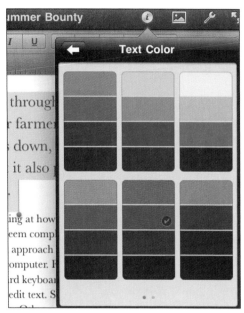

Text Color

D Scroll through the color swatches until you find one you like and tap it.

To change text color:

1. Select the text whose color you want to change and Tap ⓘ in the toolbar.

2. Tap Style in the popover, and scroll to the bottom to tap Text Options Ⓐ.

3. Tap the Color section in the Text Options panel Ⓑ. Scroll through the color swatches until you find one you like, and tap it Ⓓ.

4. If you want to change another text option, tap the Size or Font sections. If the color is the only thing you want to change, tap anywhere outside the popover to return to your document.

To change text font:

1. Select the text whose font you want to change and Tap **ⓘ** in the toolbar.

2. Tap Style in the popover, and scroll to the bottom to tap Text Options **Ⓐ**.

3. Tap the Font section in the Text Options panel **Ⓑ**. Scroll through the font family listings until you find one you like. If a font family includes several typefaces, you'll see a blue arrow on the right **Ⓔ**. Tap the arrow to choose among the typefaces. Tap a typeface to apply it.

4. If you want to change another text option, tap the top-left arrow twice to get back to the Text Options panel. If the font is the only thing you want to change, tap anywhere outside the popover to return to your document **Ⓕ**.

Ⓔ If a font family includes several typefaces, tap the blue arrow on the right to choose among them.

Not Berry Good

Wet weather throughout the spring cut both ways for farmers. It kept temperatures down, allowing better ripening. But it also pushed back to-market dates.

Let's start by looking at how to select and

Ⓕ Tap anywhere outside the popover to return to your reformatted document.

In Season This Week:

1. Obsidian blackberries

A When you reach the end of the first list line, tap the screen Return key (or press Return/Enter on an external keyboard).

In Season This Week:

1. Obsidian blackberries

2. |

B The cursor starts a new paragraph and automatically adds the next number or letter in the list sequence.

Working with Lists

Lists are great for organizing information, and Pages for iPad makes it a tap-and-go affair.

To create a list:

1. Tap where you want to begin your list.

2. Type 1, period, space (**1.**) or A, period, space (**A.**). Then type in the first list item.

3. Tap the screen Return key at the end of the line (or press Return/Enter if you're using an external keyboard) **A**. The next list number or letter in the sequence appears **B**.

4. Repeat to add as many items as needed.

5. To end the list, double-tap the screen Return key (or press Return/Enter twice if you're using an external keyboard).

To reformat a list:

1. Select a list you want to reformat **C**, or some plain text lines you want formatted as a list **D**.

2. Tap **ⓘ** in the toolbar, tap the List tab, and tap the style you want applied **E**. The list is reformatted **F**, **G**.

In Season This Week:
1. Obsidian blackberries
2. Rainier cherries
3. Bing cherries
4. raspberries
5. loganberries
6. strawberries (only a few)
7. salmon (local troll caught)

C Select a list you want to reformat.

Coming Next Week:

yellow cherry tomatoes

curly-leaf spinach

big-leaf basil

D You also can select plain text lines you want formatted as a list.

Style   List   Layout

None
• Bullet   ✓
~ Image
A. Lettered
1. Numbered

E Tap **ⓘ** in the toolbar, tap the List tab, and tap the style you want applied.

In Season This Week:
• Obsidian blackberries
• Rainier cherries
• Bing cherries
• raspberries
• loganberries
• strawberries (only a few)
• salmon (local troll caught)

F The previously numbered list now uses bullets.

Coming Next Week:
• yellow cherry tomatoes
• curly-leaf spinach
• big-leaf basil

G The previously plain text is reformatted as a list.

A To realign a paragraph, tap one of the ruler's four alignment buttons.

B Tap anywhere in a paragraph whose alignment you want to change.

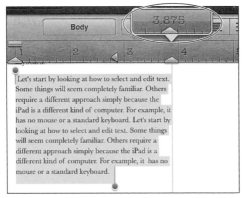

C Tap and drag the margin marker to the desired placement. As you drag the marker, a magnified readout appears.

Setting Paragraph Alignment and Margins

Pages for iPad's tools for aligning paragraphs reside in the document toolbar. You can apply any of the four choices with a single tap. You can use the ruler to set margins for selected paragraphs. Setting a document's overall margins is explained on page 30.

To change paragraph alignment:

- Tap anywhere in a paragraph whose alignment you want to change or select multiple paragraphs. Tap one of the four alignment buttons in the ruler **A**. The paragraph's text is realigned.

To change paragraph margins:

1. Tap anywhere in a paragraph whose alignment you want to change or select multiple paragraphs **B**.

2. Tap and drag the right or left margin markers to the desired placement. As you drag a marker, a magnified readout appears, enabling you to gauge the proper width **C**. Lift your finger at the desired paragraph width.

3. If necessary, repeat step 2, adjusting the opposite margin marker.

> **TIP** Resist any urge to use individual paragraph margins or Returns to accommodate nearby images or shapes. Pages for iPad has some great tools for arranging text with images and shapes. See "Arranging Objects with Text" on page 89.

To change the first-line indent:

1. Tap anywhere in a paragraph whose alignment you want to change or select multiple paragraphs.

2. Tap and drag the small rectangular marker just above the left-hand margin marker to the desired placement. As you drag a marker, a magnified readout appears, enabling you to gauge the proper indent 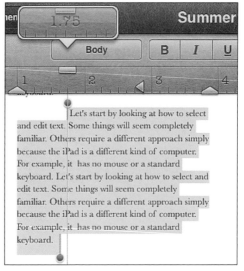. Lift your finger at the desired indent.

D Set the first-line indent by dragging the small rectangular marker, using the magnified readout to guide you.

A After tapping within a paragraph, add a tab stop by tapping anywhere along the ruler.

B To delete a tab stop, tap and hold it in the ruler (left), then drag it down off the ruler (right).

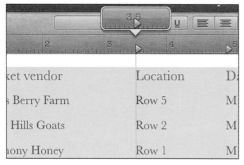

C Select multiple lines, tap and drag a tab stop and...

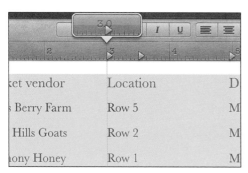

D ...all the lines move to the same spot.

Setting Tab Stops

Adding tab stops within paragraphs makes it easier to keep columns of type aligned as you type. When you add tab stops in Pages for iPad, the touch-sensitive screen is, well, sensitive. It's easy to mistakenly add an extra tab stop while trying to move an existing one.

To add a tab stop:

- Tap in the paragraph where you want to add a tab stop. Then tap anywhere in the ruler and a tab stop is added **A**. Repeat to add as many tab stops as needed.

To delete a tab stop:

- Tap a tab stop in the ruler and drag it down off the ruler **B**. Lift your finger and the tab stop is deleted.

To reposition a tab stop:

- Tap and hold any tab stop in the ruler, then drag it to a new position.

TIP By selecting multiple lines or paragraphs first, you can reposition all their tab stops at the same time **C**, **D**.

To change the tab-stop type:

1. Double-tap a default, left-aligned tab stop in the ruler to change it to a center-aligned tab stop 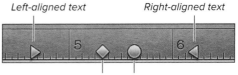.

2. Double-tap a diamond-shaped, center-aligned tab stop to change it to a right-aligned tab stop .

3. Double-tap a right-aligned tab stop to change it to a circular, decimal-aligned tab stop .

4. Double-tap a circular, decimal-aligned tab stop to change it back to a default, left-aligned-text tab stop .

TIP You can quickly change the style and alignment of tab stops in text using the same steps described in "To copy and paste a style" on page 55 , , .

To move from tab stop to tab stop:

- The iPad screen keyboard has no Tab key, so press ⇥ in the right side of the toolbar.

- If you're using a wireless or docked keyboard, press the Tab key.

Left-aligned text　　　*Right-aligned text*

Center-aligned text　*Decimal-aligned text*

E By default, new tab stops are left-aligned; double-tap a tab stop to change to one of the other three types.

F Select the text with the tab-stop style you want to copy and tap Copy Style.

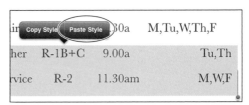

G Select text with a tab-stop style you want to change, and tap Paste Style.

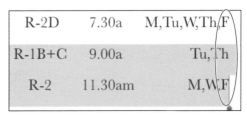

H All the text changes to the source text's tab-stop style—in this case, right-aligned.

Working with Text Columns

Like Pages for Mac, Pages for iPad does a nice job of helping you create and manage text columns. You can choose the number of columns, set their widths independently, and even dictate where to break off a column and flow the remaining text into a new column.

To set the number of columns:

1. Select the text whose column layout you want to change.
2. Tap ❶ in the toolbar, tap Layout in the popover, and then choose the number of columns you want ❹. The selected text reflows ❸.

> **TIP** You can reflow multiple pages into columns by tapping at the top of the page in step 1. You control the number of pages affected by inserting a page break where you want the reflow to stop.

❹ Tap Layout in the popover and choose the number of columns you want used.

In Season This Week:	• strawberries (only a few)
• Obsidian blackberries	• salmon (local troll caught)
• Rainier cherries	Coming Next Week:
• Bing cherries	• yellow cherry tomatoes
• raspberries	• curly-leaf spinach
• loganberries	• big-leaf basil

❸ The selected text reflows into your new column layout.

To adjust column width:

1. Tap in the column you want to resize.

2. Tap and drag the column-margin markers in the ruler **C**. The margin grows wider or narrower as desired **D**.

TIP You can independently adjust the width of a page's columns.

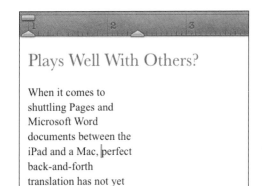

Plays Well With Others?

When it comes to
shuttling Pages and
Microsoft Word
documents between the
iPad and a Mac, perfect
back-and-forth
translation has not yet

C Tap and drag the column-margin markers to resize the column.

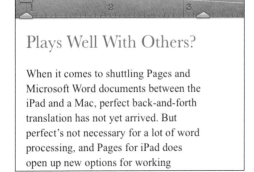

Plays Well With Others?

When it comes to shuttling Pages and
Microsoft Word documents between the
iPad and a Mac, perfect back-and-forth
translation has not yet arrived. But
perfect's not necessary for a lot of word
processing, and Pages for iPad does
open up new options for working

D The column width changes as desired.

Plays Well With Others?

When it comes to shuttling Pages and
Microsoft Word documents between the
iPad and a Mac, perfect back-and-forth
translation has not yet arrived. But
perfect's not necessary for a lot of word
processing, and Pages for iPad does
open up new options for working
beyond the office desk. As Pages for
iPad is updated, surely some of bumps
will be smoothed out—at least between
it and Pages for Mac. In the meantime,
you can sidestep some problems by
knowing where the translation process
stumbles.

Fonts: With support for more than 40
fonts and font families, the iPad does a

🅔 Tap where
you want to
force the text to
the top of the
next column.

To insert a column break in text:

1. Tap in the column where you want to
   force the text to the top of the next
   column 🅔.

2. Tap ⟶ in the toolbar and tap Column
   Break in the popover 🅕. Text appearing
   after the spot tapped in step 1 is forced
   to the top of the next column 🅖.

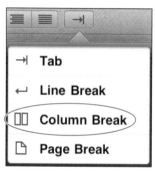

⟶ **Tab**

↵ **Line Break**

▯▯ **Column Break**

▯ **Page Break**

🅕 Tap Column
Break in the
popover.

Plays Well With Others?

When it comes to shuttling Pages and
Microsoft Word documents between the
iPad and a Mac, perfect back-and-forth
translation has not yet arrived. But
perfect's not necessary for a lot of word
processing, and Pages for iPad does
open up new options for working

Fonts: With
fonts and fo
decent subs
encounters
else. But it'
example, th
perhaps the
planet. But
and 5 in E,

🅖 Text appearing after the spot tapped is forced
to the top of the next column.

Using Page Breaks

When creating multiple-page documents, it can be very useful to insert a page break to start a new section.

To insert a page break:

- Tap in the document where you want to insert a page break. Tap ⇥ in the toolbar and tap Page Break in the popover. The break is inserted and any content below that point is forced to the next page.

To remove a page break:

1. Tap in the text just before where the content jumps to the next page. Select the hidden page-return coding between where content ends on one page and resumes on the next page Ⓐ.

2. Tap Cut in the pop-up bar or press Backspace on your screen keyboard or Delete on an external keyboard. The page break is removed Ⓑ.

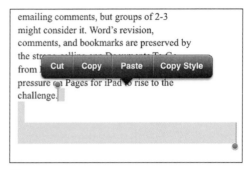

emailing comments, but groups of 2-3 might consider it. Word's revision, comments, and bookmarks are preserved by the st___ ___ ___ ___ ___ ___ from ___ pressure on Pages for iPad to rise to the challenge.

| Cut | Copy | Paste | Copy Style |

Ⓐ Select the always hidden page-return coding between where content ends on one page and resumes on the next page.

emailing comments, but groups of 2-3 might consider it. Word's revision, comments, and bookmarks are preserved by the strong-selling app Documents To Go, from DataViz. Hopefully that puts some pressure on Pages for iPad to rise to the challenge. There are three ways to get documents in and out of Pages for iPad. You can use iTunes to shift files from your iPad to your Mac over the included USB cable. You can share them with other iWork users logged into the iWork.com public

Ⓑ After you delete the hidden coding, the page break is removed.

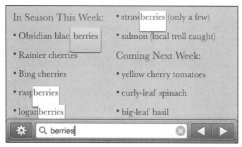

A To search for a word, tap Find in the popover.

B Search results are immediately highlighted in the document.

C You refine your search by searching for matching cases or whole words only. Or, simply tap Find and Replace.

Using Text Tools

Pages for iPad comes with the standard text tools: find and replace, check spelling, and a dictionary for when you're stumped about word choice.

To find text:

1. Tap 🔧 in the toolbar and tap Find in the popover **A**.

2. When the search field appears at the bottom of the screen, type in the word(s) you're searching for. The results are immediately highlighted in the document **B**. Use the forward and back arrows to move through the document to see the results in context.

3. To replace the found term, tap 🔅 to the left of the search field.

4. In the popover, you can refine your search by searching for matching cases or whole words only **C**. Or, simply tap Find and Replace and a second text field appears to the right of the search field.

Continues on next page

5. Type in the replacement word and tap Replace. Pages for iPad finds the first instance of the word and replaces it . Tap the forward and back arrows to find each instance and manually replace it by tapping the Replace button.

6. To automatically find and replace all instances of the word, tap and hold the Replace button until Replace All appears in the popover **E**. Tap it and all the found words are automatically replaced.

D Tap Replace; Pages for iPad finds the first instance of the word and replaces it.

E To automatically find and replace all instances of the word, tap and hold Replace until Replace All appears.

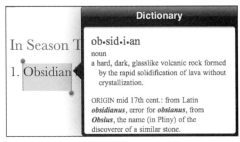

F To look up a word, double-tap it. Tap More in the first pop-up bar, and then tap Definition.

G The Dictionary popover appears, displaying the word's meaning and origins.

To turn on/off auto spell check:

- Tap 🔧 in the toolbar and slide the Check Spelling button on or off **A**. With it on, misspelled words are underlined in red.

To look up a word:

- Double-tap a word to select it, tap More in the pop-up bar, and then tap Definition **F**. The Dictionary popover appears, displaying the word's meaning and origins **G**. Tap anywhere on the screen to close the popover.

Putting It All Together

1. Show and hide both the document toolbar and the ruler.

2. Select some text and change its style, size, color, and font family.

3. Copy a style from one selection and paste it to another.

4. Create a numbered text list, then change it to a bulleted list.

5. Change the alignment of one paragraph, then select another paragraph and give it an alignment different from the first.

6. Create a set of tab stops that use all four types, then apply those settings to either new or existing text.

7. Select a page of single-column text and apply a two- or three-column layout.

8. Apply two different widths to your two- or three-column layout.

9. Insert a page break somewhere within that layout and, if necessary, adjust the text flow to work well with the break.

Working with Images and Shapes

In any document, text bears the informational burden. But the document's visual variety helps keep us engaged. Pages for iPad makes it easy to add images, text boxes, and shapes to do just that.

In This Chapter

Importing Images

You need to move images onto your iPad before you can insert them in your pages. You have two routes for doing that: Using iTunes to sync photos from your main computer or using the Camera Connection Kit, sold separately by Apple.

To sync images with iTunes:

1. Connect the iPad to your computer and open iTunes. Select your iPad when it appears in the left column of iTunes.

2. Click the Photos tab and select the "Sync Photos from" check box. By default, iPhoto is selected, along with the Include videos check box. (See Tip.) If you don't want to copy all your iPhoto images over to the iPad, click "Selected albums, events, and faces" and select among the albums listed .

3. Once you've made your choices, click Sync at the bottom right of iTunes **B**. The computer's photos are copied to your iPad.

4. Back on your iPad, switch to Pages to insert any of the images into your documents.

TIP If you switch your "Sync Photos from" setting to something other than iPhoto—for example, an individual folder—all the iPhoto photos are deleted from the iPad in the next sync. I've not found a workaround for this.

A Click the Photos tab and select the "Sync Photos from" check box.

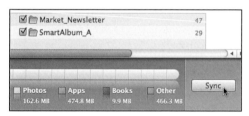

B Once you've made your choices, click Sync at the bottom right of iTunes.

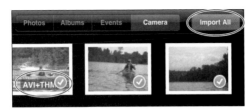

C The iPad's Photos app shows all the images to be imported, including videos (left). Tap Import All.

D If the import contains images already on the iPad, tap Skip Duplicates.

E Once the import's finished, always tap Keep.

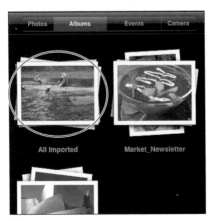

F The Photos app switches to the Albums tab, where the newly imported images appear in a stack.

To import images with the Camera Connection Kit:

1. Attach a USB cable from your camera or iPhone to the kit's Camera Connector. Plug the connector into the iPad port.

   or

   Insert an SD card into the kit's SD Card Reader. Plug the reader into the iPad port.

2. The iPad's Photos app opens and displays all the images to be imported. Tap Import All **C**. Or, tap individual images and videos you want to import and tap Import.

3. If the import contains images already on the iPad, tap Skip Duplicates **D**.

4. Once the import is finished, always tap Keep **E**. (See Tip.)

5. Tap the Photos app's Albums tab, which shows the newly imported images as a stack **F**.

6. Remove the Camera Connector or SD Card Reader from the iPad port.

7. Switch to Pages to insert any of the images into your documents.

TIP In step 4, never tap Delete. If you do, the images are wiped off the connected card or camera. It's always best to do this back on your camera—once you're dead sure everything imported correctly.

Inserting Images and Video

Pages for iPad makes it easy to use any of the photos stored by your iPad's Photos app. Be sure to do any photo editing, such as exposure adjustment, on your main computer.

To insert an image:

1. Tap on the page in the general area where you want to insert an image.

2. Tap 🖼, tap the Media tab, and tap the photo album containing the image you want to use **A**.

3. Scroll through the album thumbnails until you find the desired image, then tap it **B**. The image is inserted on the page **C**. Don't worry if it's not exactly where you want it. (See Tip.)

TIP When inserting images into text, it's common for the image to appear in not quite the right spot. You can easily reposition it. (See "To move an object" on page 79.) Also, be aware that, by default, an image repositions itself as you add or delete text above it. (See "To control how objects move with text" on page 99.)

TIP Pages for iPad saves the inserted image as part of the document. Even if you delete the original image from the Photos app's albums, the inserted image remains.

A To insert an image, tap 🖼, tap the Media tab, and tap a photo album.

B Scroll through the album thumbnails and tap the image you want to use.

C The selected image appears on the page.

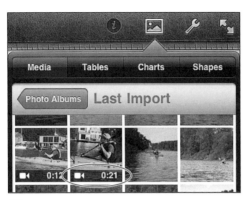

D Tap the thumbnail of the video you want to insert; videos are marked by a movie camera icon.

E The selected image appears on the page.

F A progress bar appears as the video is compressed.

To insert a video:

1. Tap on the page in the general area you want to insert a video.

2. Tap ![icon], tap the Media tab, and tap the photo album containing the video you want to use.

3. Scroll through the album thumbnails until you find the desired video, then tap it **D**.

4. When the video preview appears, tap Use **E**.

5. A progress bar appears beneath the preview as the video is compressed **F**. The video is then inserted in the page **G**, where you can move and resize it as needed.

TIP Pages for iPad saves the inserted video as part of the document. Even if you delete the original video from the Photos app's albums, the inserted video remains.

G Once the video's inserted on the page, you can move and resize it.

To delete an image or video:

1. Tap the image or video once, and the blue handles appear.

2. Wait a moment, and tap it lightly once more in the center (not on the handles). A pop-up bar appears, which includes a Delete option.

3. Tap Delete and the image or video is removed from the page.

TIP Think of this two-step tap as a slow double-tap. If you don't wait a moment between taps, the pop-up bar won't appear.

H To delete an image or video, tap it once. Wait a moment, tap it again, and the pop-up bar with the Delete option appears.

A As you move an object, yellow guidelines and x,y coordinates appear to help you align it with the rest of the layout.

Moving and Resizing Objects

In this section, the examples show how to move and resize images. Whether you're working with text boxes, shapes, charts, or tables, however, the steps are the same since Pages for iPad treats them all as objects.

To move an object:

1. Tap the object you want to move. When it's selected, blue "handles" appear around the edge.

2. Tap and hold the object, then drag it to its new position. Yellow guidelines and x,y coordinates appear to help you align the object with the rest of the layout **A**.

3. Lift your finger and the object is repositioned.

To resize an object:

1. Tap the object you want to resize **B**.

2. Drag any blue "handle" around the object's edge to resize it **C**. Drag toward the center to make the object smaller, or away from the center to enlarge it.

3. Lift your finger and tap anywhere on the screen to apply the resizing. You may need to reposition the object **D**. (See Tip.)

TIP In the default settings, text surrounding the object may reflow as it's resized. To stop this, see "To control how objects move with text" on page 99.

B Tap the object to select it.

C Drag any blue handle inward or outward to resize the image.

D You may need to reposition the object after it's resized.

In Season This Week: Coming Next
• Obsidian   ⟨Done⟩ ellow cherry
• Rainier cherries   • curly-leaf spin

A Double-tap the center of an image and the mask slider appears below it.

In Season This Week: Coming Next Week:
• Obsidian   ⟨Done⟩ ellow cherry tomatoes
• Rainier cherries   • curly-leaf spinach
• Bing cherries   • fiddle heads

B Drag the slider to move in or out on the image. Tap Done when you finish.

In Season This Week: Coming Next
• Obsidian blackberries   • yellow cherry
• Rainier cherries   • curly-leaf spin

C The mask is applied to the photo.

Masking Images

Use Pages for iPad's masking feature to pare away the nonessential parts of an image. Unlike traditional cropping, which permanently discards the unused portion of an image, masking leaves the photo intact. The mask simply acts as an overlay (like a window) for the photo. That gives you the option of repositioning the mask at any time. If you are accustomed to using other page-layout applications, you might think of masking as scaling.

To mask an image:

1. Double-tap the center of the image you want to mask and a slider appears below it **A**.

2. Drag the slider to move in or out on the image within the overlay mask **B**. If you need to reframe the mask, tap and drag the image.

3. Tap Done when you finish. The mask is applied to the photo **C**.

> **TIP** If you use the mask to move all the way in—thereby increasing the scale of the image— make sure the photo still looks sharp. Low-resolution cameras, such as those on early cell phones, may not capture enough detail to support full zoom. In that case, just move the slider left to the point where the photo looks reasonably crisp.

Flipping Images

Pages for iPad gives you the option to flip images vertically (upside down) or horizontally (right to left). This only works for images, not text boxes, shapes, charts, or tables.

To flip an image:

1. Tap the image you want to flip .

2. Tap ⓘ, tap the Arrange tab, and tap Flip Vertically or Flip Horizontally ⓑ. The image flips based on your choice ⓒ.

Ⓐ Tap the image you want to flip.

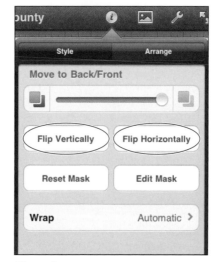

Ⓑ Tap ⓘ, tap the Arrange tab, and choose which way to flip the image.

Ⓒ The image flipped horizontally (left) or vertically (right).

Adding Background Images

Pages for iPad gives you the option of adding background images to documents. (This option is not available on a page-by-page basis.) Used with restraint, the ability to add background images makes it easy to create stationery for special purposes. The steps combine what you've learned so far in this chapter with the document setup tasks covered in Chapter 3.

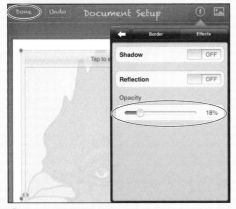

Ⓐ In the Document Setup view, tap the Media tab and insert a background image.

Ⓑ Move the Opacity slider to less than 20 percent. Tap Done to close the Document Setup view.

Ⓒ In the My Documents view, rename the document to signal its purpose.

1. Create a new blank document as explained on page 24.

2. Open the document and tap the 🔧 in the toolbar, and then tap Document Setup in the popover.

3. In the Document Setup view, tap 🖼, tap the Media tab, and insert a background image Ⓐ. (For more information, see page 76.)

4. Double-tap the image to move, resize, and mask it as needed. (For more information, see pages 79 and 81.)

5. Tap ⓘ and tap Style Options in the Style tab.

6. Move the Opacity slider to less than 20 percent (lighter is often better) to fade back the page-size image Ⓑ. Tap Done to close the Document Setup view.

7. In the My Documents view, rename the document to help you remember its purpose Ⓒ.

8. When the need arises, duplicate the document and add in your new content Ⓓ. (For more information, see page 28.)

Ⓓ When you need it, duplicate the document and add in your special-purpose content.

Adding Text Boxes

Use text boxes whenever you want to create a bit of text that is not part of the document's body text. For example, you may want to add captions, callouts, or sidebars that can be positioned outside the main text flow.

To insert a text box:

1. Tap on the page in the general area you want to insert a text box.

2. Tap ![icon], tap the Shapes tab, and drag the boxed T onto the page Ⓐ.

3. When the text box appears on the page, drag it into position on the page.

4. Double-tap the text box and begin typing Ⓑ. You can also paste text cut or copied from elsewhere. Your text appears within the box Ⓒ.

Ⓐ To insert a text box, tap the Shapes tab, and drag the boxed T onto the page.

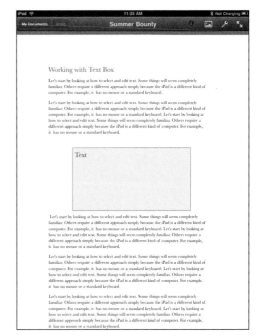

Ⓑ When the text box appears on the page, double-tap it, and begin typing.

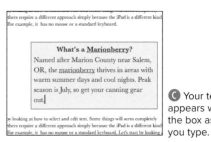

Ⓒ Your text appears within the box as you type.

season is July, so get your canning gear out. By the way, the marionberry is

⊞

at how to select and edit text. Some things will seem completely

D If you type in more text than the present box will hold, a + button appears at the bottom edge. Just tap the box and resize it.

thers require a different approach simply because the iPad is
For
rd
how to
seem
uire a
e iPad
For
rd

by
xt.

pproach
kind of
use or a
king at
things
thers
imply
nd of
use or a

by
xt. Some

thers require a different approach simply because the iPad is

What's a Marionberry?

Named after Marion County near Salem, OR, the marionberry thrives in areas with warm summer days and cool nights.

Peak season is July, so get your canning gear out. By the way, the marionberry is actually a type of blackberry. Folks love its sweet, but not-too-sweet quality.

example
keyboa
select a
comple
differer
is a dif
examp
keyboa

looking
Some
familia
simply
compu
standa
how to
will se
require
becaus
compu
standa

looking
things wil

E Various headings, styles, and alignments can be applied to any text box.

TIP If you type in more text than the present box holds, a + button appears at the bottom edge **D**. Tap the box and resize it by dragging the blue handles.

TIP Various headings, styles, and alignments can be applied to any text-box content **E**.

TIP Just like images, text boxes will shift around on the page as you add or delete text above them. To prevent this, see "To control how objects move with text" on page 99.

Inserting Shapes

While you can use shapes purely for decoration, they also can act as text boxes. In either case, Pages for iPad gives you choices for styling and formatting shapes.

To insert a shape:

1. Tap on the page in the general area you want to insert a shape.

2. Tap 🖼, tap the Shapes tab, and drag a shape onto the page Ⓐ.

3. When the shape appears on the page, tap and drag it into position as needed.

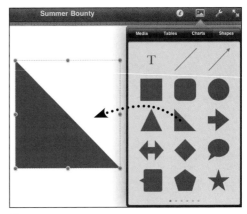

Ⓐ In the Shapes tab, tap and drag a shape onto the page.

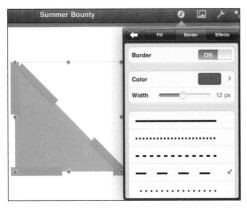

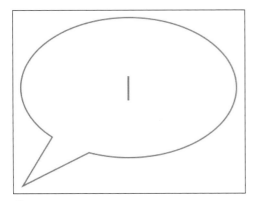

B A variety of style options, such as fills, borders, and effects, can be applied to any shape.

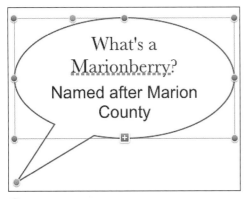

C To use a shape as a text box, double-tap the center and begin typing.

What's a
Marionberry?
Named after Marion
County

D You also can paste in text you've copied from elsewhere.

4. With the shape selected, tap **ⓘ**, then tap the Style tab to change the fill, border, or effects **B**.

or

If you want to use a shape as a text box, double-tap the center and begin typing **C**. Or, paste text you've copied from elsewhere in your document **D**. (See "To control how objects move with text" on page 99.)

TIP If you type in more text than the shape holds, a + button appears at the bottom edge. Tap the shape and resize it by dragging the blue handles **E**. Or, resize the text itself.

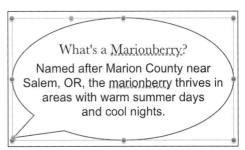

What's a Marionberry?
Named after Marion County near
Salem, OR, the marionberry thrives in
areas with warm summer days
and cool nights.

E Resize the text or increase the box size to fit all the text.

Putting It All Together

1. Use iTunes to move some images and a video to your iPad.

2. Insert one of those images into a Pages for iPad document.

3. Insert a video into the same document.

4. Select, move, and resize an image in a document.

5. Apply a mask to an image.

6. Flip an image that you've inserted on a page.

7. Using a new document, add a background image to its pages.

8. Insert a text box on a page, add text to it, and then style that text.

9. Insert two different shapes on a page. Style one as a decorative element; use the other as a text box.

Arranging Objects and Text

A Pages for iPad document is the sum of all its parts: text and headers, images, shapes, charts, and tables. In that sense, this chapter is the heart of Pages for iPad. Here's where you learn how to arrange all those parts on the page so they work together.

Arranging Objects

Thanks to the iPad's touch screen, Pages for iPad includes a bunch of ways to move and group objects. The nudge motion—and its multi-fingered variations—is a good example of how gestures are used to lay out the page. (See **Table 8.1**.)

To nudge objects:

1. Touch an object on the screen and keep your finger in place 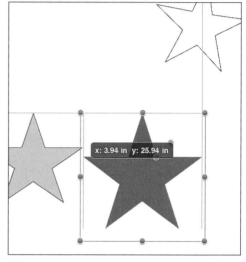. Then do any of the following:

   ▸ Swipe another finger (either hand) up or down on the screen to move the object. The object moves one pixel in that direction (though the x,y coordinates readout only displays inches).

   ▸ Swipe two fingers in the direction you want to move the object. The object moves 10 pixels in that direction.

   ▸ Swipe three fingers in the direction you want to move the object. The object moves 20 pixels in that direction.

   ▸ Swipe four fingers in the direction you want to move the object. The object moves 30 pixels in that direction.

TABLE 8.1 Pixel Pushing

Use This Many Fingers	To Move Object This Many Pixels
1	1
2	10
3	20
4	30

x: 3.94 in   y: 25.94 in

Ⓐ To nudge an object, touch it on the screen and keep your finger in place.

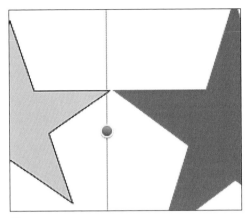

B With repeated nudges, you can put an object exactly where you want it.

2. Repeat any of the gestures in any direction to move the object to exactly where you want it **B**.

TIP It's tricky sometimes to select the object and not wind up triggering a text cursor, the magnifying glass, or a pop-up bar. Just tap well outside the object to start over.

TIP If the Edge Guides are turned on, they appear when you select the object, displaying thin yellow lines to aid in alignment with nearby objects **A**.

TIP You cannot move objects diagonally using a finger swipe—just up or down.

TIP If you select multiple objects, you can then tap and hold your finger on the objects and then move the group.

To select more than one object:

1. Touch an object on the screen and keep your finger in place. The object is selected when its blue selection handles appear **C**.

2. Without lifting the first finger, tap the other objects you want to select. All are selected, as indicated by the selection handles **D**. You can now move them together.

TIP If the selected objects are all the same type (shapes or images, for example), you can restyle them all at once **E**.

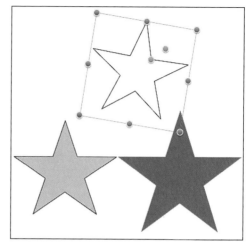

C Start by selecting a single object.

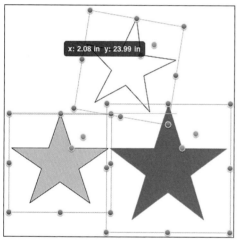

x: 2.08 in y: 23.99 in

D Tap other objects to add them to the selection.

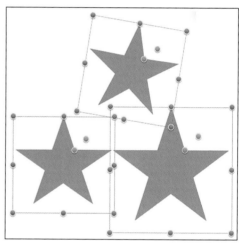

E If the selected objects are the same type, you can restyle them all at once.

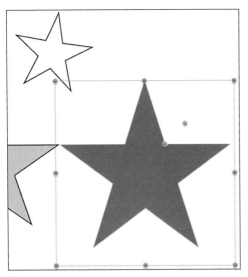

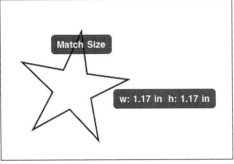

To match the size of objects:

1. Tap to select the first object whose size you want to change, and start dragging any of the blue selection handles **F**.

2. Use your other hand to tap the second object whose size you want to match. The words Match Size appear very briefly, along with the size of the second object **G**. The first object resizes to match the second **H**.

> **TIP** As you can see **G**, no other aspect of the target object, such as its orientation, changes.

F Tap to select the first object whose size you want to change, and start dragging any of the blue selection handles.

G Tap the second object whose size you want to match. The words Match Size and its size in inches appear briefly.

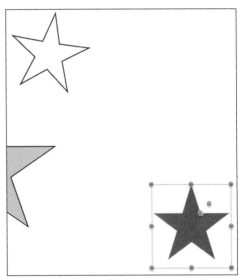

H The first object resizes to match the second.

To delete an object:

1. Tap the object, and the blue selection handles appear **I**.

2. Wait a moment, and tap it lightly once more in the center (not on the handles). A pop-up bar, which includes a Delete option, appears. **J**.

3. Tap Delete and the object is removed from the page **K**.

TIP If you don't wait a moment between taps, the pop-up bar won't appear.

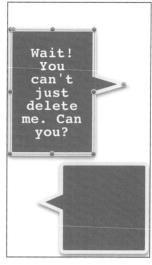

I To delete an object, tap it once and the blue selection handles appear.

J Wait a moment, tap it again, and the pop-up bar with the Delete option appears.

K Tap Delete and the object is removed from the page.

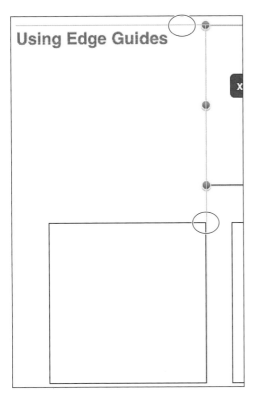

Working with Edge Guides

Pages for iPad automatically displays edge guides whenever you move an object on a page that contains other objects. The thin yellow lines respond dynamically to your actions, showing the edges of other objects as you drag the first. If they interfere with your view, it's easy to turn them off.

To use edge guides:

- Tap and drag an object to reposition it. As you do, the edge guides show you the edges of other objects on the page Ⓐ. Use them to guide your positioning of the selected object.

TIP Pages for iPad displays yellow lines to mark the centers of nearby objects as well.

To turn off edge guides:

- Tap 🔧 in the toolbar, and slide the Edge Guides button to OFF Ⓑ.

TIP To restore the edge guides, tap 🔧 and slide the Edge Guides button back to ON.

TIP The center guides are not affected by the setting and cannot be turned off.

Ⓐ Use the yellow edge guides to help drag selected objects into position.

Ⓑ To turn off the edge guides, tap 🔧 and slide the Edge Guides button to OFF.

Stacking Objects

Pages for iPad lets you stack, or layer, objects so that one appears on top of another. You also can change the stack order.

To stack or layer objects:

1. Tap to select the first object and drag it toward another object **A**. Depending on each object's settings, the first object glides over or under the second object **B**. To change its position in the stack, see the next two tasks.

To reverse the stacking order of two objects:

1. Tap either object to select it.
2. Tap **i** in the toolbar, and tap the Arrange tab **C**.
3. Drag the slider to the opposite side. The stack order reverses **D**.

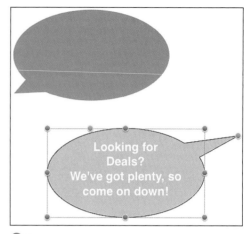

A Tap and drag the selected object toward another object.

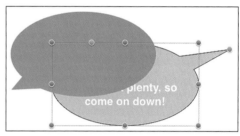

B Depending on each object's settings, the first glides over or under the second.

C Tap **i** in the toolbar, and tap the Arrange tab.

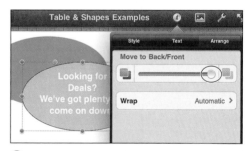

D Drag the slider to the opposite side to reverse the stack order.

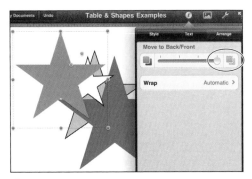

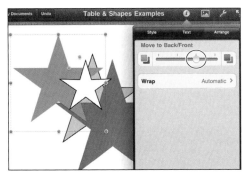

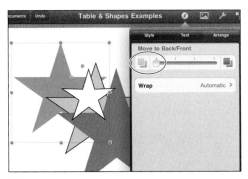

E The selected object sits at the top of stack, with the slider button at the far right.

F Move the slider one tick to the left to drop the object down one layer.

G Tap the button at the far left to put the object at the bottom of the stack.

To rearrange a stack of multiple objects:

1. In a stack of overlapping objects, tap the object whose order in the stack you want to change.

2. Tap **ⓘ** in the toolbar, and tap the Arrange tab. The slider button shows the position of the selected object relative to the rest of the stack. In our example, the object sits at the top of stack, with the slider button at the far right **E**.

3. Move the slider one tick to the left to drop the object down one layer **F**. Or, tap the button at the far left to put the object at the bottom of the stack **G**.

4. Select any other objects in the stack, and use the slider to change their positions as needed.

TIP Larger objects near the top of the stack can make it hard to select smaller objects lower in the stack. The solution: Select the larger object and move it down the stack order until you're able to select the smaller object.

TIP The number of ticks along the slider equals the number of objects in the stack.

Arranging Objects with Text

By default, Pages for iPad automatically wraps text around objects, whether they are images, shapes, or text boxes. However, you can change that using the Arrange tab.

Objects with "Move with Text" turned off behave much like what Pages for Mac and many layout programs call "floating" objects. As such, they move independently of nearby text. When you toggle "Move with Text" on for a selected object, it's placed "inline" with the text so that they stick together in the layout.

To wrap text around objects:

1. Tap to select the object for which you want to control the surrounding text flow.

2. Tap 🛈 in the toolbar, tap the Arrange tab, and tap the Wrap slider, which by default is set to Automatic .

3. Depending on how the object and text were wrapped at the start, tap Around or Above and Below ⓑ. (See Tip.) The text repositions based on your choice ⓒ.

> **TIP** The Automatic setting represents Pages for iPad's best guess at the optimum layout. Depending on the selected object, however, there may be no difference between it and Around or Above and Below. For example, in figure ⓑ the Automatic setting already put the surrounding text above and below the object.

> **TIP** Don't try this at home! The ⓒ and ⓓ text-wrap screen shots are meant as easy-to-see examples, not a typographic endorsement. In reality, creating a gap this big in the text would make it very hard for anyone to read it. Instead, you would do better to use a small object that doesn't interrupt the text flow or, even better, place the object along the text's edge. That way, the text can gently flow around the object without becoming unreadable.

ⓐ Tap the Arrange tab and tap the Wrap slider, set by default to Automatic.

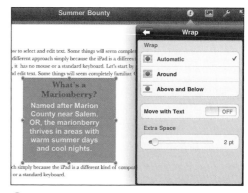

ⓑ Depending on how the object and text were wrapped at the start, tap Around or Above and Below.

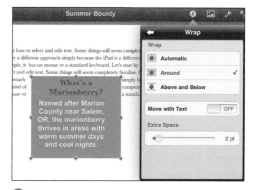

ⓒ The text repositions based on your choice, in this case, Around.

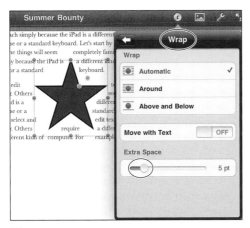

To adjust the space between an object and text:

1. Tap to select the object for which you want to adjust the surrounding space.

2. Tap **ⓘ** in the toolbar and tap the Arrange tab. Then tap the Wrap slider to reach the Wrap panel with the Extra Space slider **ⓓ**.

3. Drag the Extra Space slider to leave more or less space between the object and the text **ⓔ**.

4. Tap anywhere on the screen to apply the change.

To control how objects move with text:

1. Tap **ⓘ** in the toolbar and tap the Arrange tab. Then tap the Wrap slider to reach the Wrap panel.

2. Drag the Move with Text slider to ON **ⓕ**.

3. Tap anywhere on the screen to apply the change. Now, when you move the surrounding text, the object moves with the text. (See Tip.)

ⓓ Use the Extra Space slider to change the space between the object and text.

ⓔ Moving the slider to the right increases the space between the object and text.

ⓕ To keep an object and its surrounding text together, drag the Move with Text slider to ON.

TIP This works reliably in Pages for Mac, but getting it to work right in Pages for iPad has been very buggy. When I can't drag the object and text together, I select them together, then cut and paste the whole selection to a new location. To see if a better workaround has been found, search the Web for "Move with Text" + "Pages for iPad." Or go to this book's companion website to learn more.

Putting It All Together

1. Select an object and nudge it using one, two, three, and four fingers.

2. Select two or three objects at once.

3. Match the size of two objects.

4. Use the edge guides to help you reposition one object in relation to others on the page.

5. Turn off the edge guides and reposition objects on the page without them.

6. Create a stack of three overlapping objects.

7. Change the stack order of the three objects.

8. Place an object amid text and change the default text flow.

9. Adjust the amount of space between an object and nearby text.

8

Working with Charts

Pages for iPad gives you lots of options for charts beyond changing their type and colors. Chart titles, legends, labels, numbers—and their related font and size options—can all be customized with a few taps. Charts can be moved, resized, stacked, and arranged like all other objects in Pages for iPad. (For more information, see "Arranging Objects and Text" on page 89.)

In This Chapter

Adding Charts

Adding a chart to a Pages for iPad document is simple and direct. What's more complicated is deciding which chart type to use and how to format it. Fortunately, it's easy to change the chart type at any time. (For more on that, see "To change the chart type" on page 105.)

To add a chart:

1. Tap on the page in the general area where you want to add a chart.

2. Tap  and tap the Charts tab to choose a chart type **A**.

3. Swipe through the six panels of color variations for the nine chart types. When you find one that suits your needs, tap it, and it's inserted on the page **B**.

4. Double-tap the chart and it flips around so you can edit the numbers and header labels **C**.

A Tap  and tap the Charts tab to choose among nine chart types.

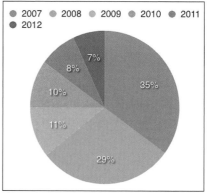

B Once you tap a chart, it's inserted on the page.

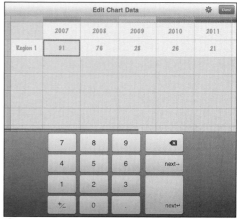

C Double-tapping the chart flips it around so you can edit the numbers and header labels.

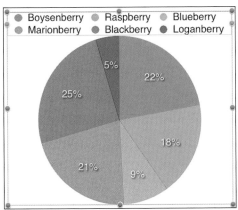

D Tap a cell's number or header label to change it.

Edit Chart Data ⚙ Done

ʳry	Marionberry	Blackberry	Loganberry
	26	21	18

E Click Done to apply the changes.

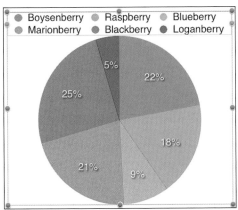

- Boysenberry ● Raspberry ● Blueberry
- Marionberry ● Blackberry ● Loganberry

F The Edit Chart Data view closes and returns you to the page view of the edited chart.

5. Tap a cell's number or header label to change it, using the screen calculator or keyboard, or your external keyboard **D**.

6. Click Done to apply the changes and return to the page view of the chart **E**, **F**.

TIP **By default, the pie chart numbers are displayed as percentages.**

Adding or Deleting Columns and Rows

If you have more entries to make than the chart has columns or rows, it's easy to do that within the Edit Chart Data view. In fact, it's so easy to accidentally add a column or row that you may find yourself deleting those more often than you add them on purpose.

To create a new column or row:

1. When you need to create a new column or row for additional chart data, tap an empty cell at the bottom or to the right of the existing entries. Or, if you're using an external keyboard, press the Tab key.

2. Enter the new data in the cell. The previously blank header is labeled "Untitled 1" 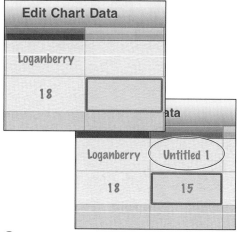 .

3. Tap the header label cell to type in a name for the untitled column or row.

To delete a column or row:

1. Double-tap the color bar above the header label cell to select the entire column or row.

2. Wait a moment after the blue selection handles appear, then tap the column or row again. Tap Delete in the pop-up bar 🅑 . The column or row is deleted.

🅐 To create a new column or row for additional data, enter the data in an empty cell at the bottom or to the right of the existing entries. The previously blank header is labeled "Untitled 1" until you give it a name.

🅑 To delete a column or row, double-tap it. Wait a moment to tap it again, and then tap Delete in the pop-up bar.

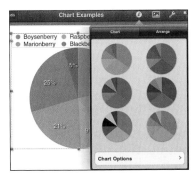

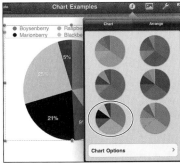

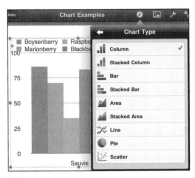

A To change a selected chart's colors, tap **ⓘ** in the toolbar, and tap the Charts tab.

B Tap one of the six color schemes to apply it to the chart.

C To change the chart type, select the chart and tap another choice in the Chart Options panel.

D Make a choice in the Chart Options panel, and the chart switches to that chart type.

Changing Chart Colors or Types

Pages for iPad makes it easy to change your mind if you add a chart, start filling it, and then realize it's not right for your purposes. Instead of starting all over, you can simply switch to another color combination or chart type.

To change the chart colors:

1. Tap the chart you want to change. Tap **ⓘ** in the toolbar, and then tap the Charts tab **A**.

2. Tap one of the six color schemes to apply it to the chart **B**. Close the tab by tapping anywhere on the screen.

To change the chart type:

1. Tap the chart you want to change. Tap **ⓘ** in the toolbar, tap the Charts tab, and then tap Chart Options **C**.

2. In the Chart Options panel, tap another choice. The chart switches to your choice **D**. If you're satisfied with the change, tap anywhere on the screen, or tap another chart choice.

TIP In step 1, be sure to tap **ⓘ**. If you mistakenly tap 🖼, you wind up generating a *new* chart rather than changing the existing chart. In that case, tap Undo in the document toolbar.

Changing Titles and Legends

By default, a chart's title (heading) and legend (or key) occupy the same top-center spot. If you have both turned on, it's hard to read either. The title cannot be moved, so if you want to use both, you have to move the legend. The title and legend also share text size and font settings, which cannot be set independently.

To add a title:

1. Tap the chart you want to change. Tap ℹ in the toolbar, tap the Charts tab, and then tap Chart Options.

2. In the Chart Options panel, tap the Chart Title button to switch it to On 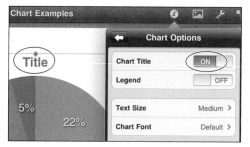. Placeholder text for the title appears.

3. Tap the placeholder text once, wait a moment, and then double-tap it. A cursor appears, enabling you to select the text and type in a title of your choosing **B**, **C**.

TIP In our example, we used the Chart Options panel to first turn off the legend, which covered up the chart's title.

TIP You cannot change a chart title's color. However, you can change its size and font indirectly. See "To resize title and legend text" on page 108 and "To change the title and legend font" on page 109.

A Tap the Chart Title button to switch it on and display the title's placeholder text.

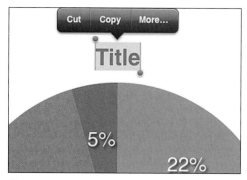

B To select the placeholder, tap it once, wait a moment, and then double-tap it. Type to replace the placeholder with your own title.

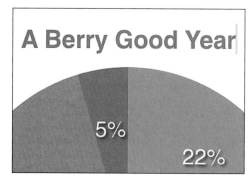

C The new title appears above the chart.

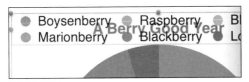

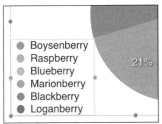

D By default, the title and legend occupy the same spot, making them hard to read if both are turned on.

E One option: Turn off the title.

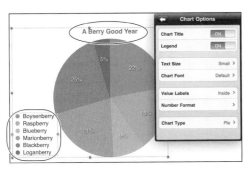

F Another option: Drag the legend to a different spot beside the chart.

G After moving the legend, the title can be turned back on and easily read.

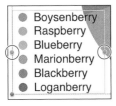

H Tap the legend, wait for the green handles to appear, and drag to resize it.

To move or resize the legend:

1. If the selected chart's title and legend are both turned on **D**, turn off the title. Tap **ⓘ**, then tap the Charts tab, and the Chart Options button.

2. In the Chart Options panel, tap the Chart Title button to switch it off **E**.

3. Tap the center of the legend and drag it from the top of the chart to another spot beside the chart **F**.

4. Now, if you like, you can turn the title back on without it interfering with the legend **G**. If necessary, you also can reduce the size of the legend's text. (See "To resize title and legend text" on page 108.)

TIP In step 3, you're not confined to placing the legend inside the current boundary, which is marked by the chart's blue selection handles. The boundary automatically expands to accommodate the larger "footprint" of a new chart-legend combination.

TIP To change the legend's shape independently of the chart, tap the legend and wait for two *green* selection handles to appear **H**. You can then change the legend's proportions without affecting the chart **I**.

I The legend resizes without affecting the chart's size or proportions.

To resize title and legend text:

1. Tap the chart you want to change. Tap ⓘ in the toolbar, tap the Charts tab, and then tap Chart Options.

2. In the Chart Options panel, tap Text Size ⓙ.

3. Change the setting to a smaller text size to reduce the legend's overall footprint ⓚ, ⓛ.

4. If necessary, reposition the legend text slightly to avoid overlapping your chart ⓜ.

ⓙ In the Chart Options panel, tap Text Size.

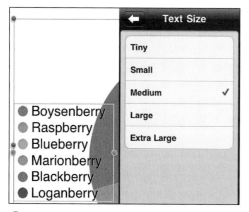

ⓚ In the Text Size panel, change the setting from Medium ...

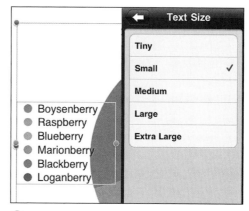

ⓛ ... to Small to reduce the legend's overall size.

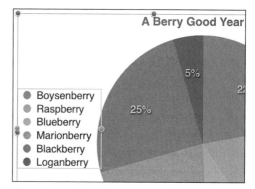

ⓜ Since text resizing alone wasn't quite enough, move the legend text slightly to the left to avoid overlapping the pie chart.

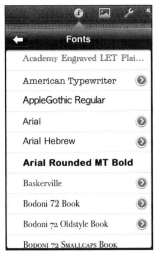

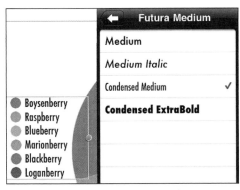

N Scroll through the font family listings; a blue arrow on the right indicates the font has several typefaces.

O Tap a typeface to apply it.

To change the title and legend font:

1. Tap the chart you want to change. Tap **ⓘ** in the toolbar, tap the Charts tab, and then tap Chart Options.

2. In the Chart Options panel, tap Chart Font **J**.

3. Scroll through the font family listings until you find one you like. If a font family includes several typefaces, there's a blue arrow on the right **N**. Tap the arrow to choose among the typefaces.

4. Tap a typeface to apply it **O**. Tap anywhere on the screen to close the panel.

Placing Value Labels

When you're ready to fine-tune your chart, the Chart Options panel allows you to adjust where the labels for values are placed.

To set value label placement:

1. Tap the chart you want to change. Tap **ⓘ** in the toolbar, tap the Charts tab, and then tap Chart Options.

2. In the Chart Options panel, tap Value Labels **Ⓐ**.

3. Choose among the four placement options or turn the labels off **Ⓑ**, **Ⓒ**.

4. Tap anywhere to exit the panel.

Ⓐ In the Chart Options panel, tap Value Labels.

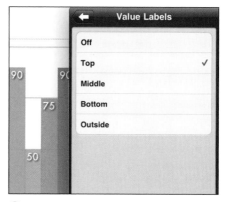

Ⓑ Choose among the four placement options, including Top.

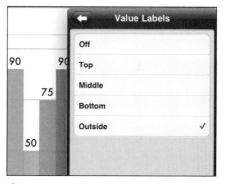

Ⓒ The Outside choice moves the labels outside the colored element.

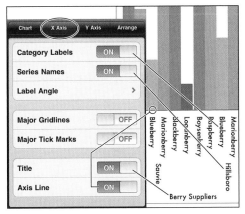

A In the X Axis tab, six buttons—four of which are turned on here—control the display of axis items.

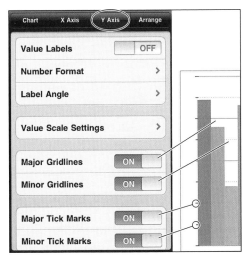

B In the Y Axis tab, five buttons—four of which are turned on here—control the display of axis items.

C The Label Angle panel offers five ways to orient the labels.

Displaying Axis Items

Pages for iPad offers so many options for labeling and formatting your chart that it would be a thicket if they were all turned on. Set separately for the X (horizontal) and Y (vertical) axes, they fall in three broad categories: labels; gridlines and tick marks; and the title and baseline for the axis itself A, B.

To show or hide X-axis items:

1. Tap the chart you want to change. Tap 🛈 in the toolbar, and then tap the X Axis tab.

2. Choose among the six options for turning on or off Category Labels, Series Names, Major Gridlines, Major Tick Marks, Title, and Axis Line A.

3. If you turn on labels, tap Label Angle to set whether labels run vertically, horizontally, or diagonally C.

4. Tap anywhere to exit the panel.

To show or hide Y-axis items:

1. Tap the chart you want to change. Tap **ⓘ** in the toolbar, and then tap the Y Axis tab.

2. Choose among the five options for turning on or off Value Labels, Major Gridlines, Minor Gridlines, Major Tick Marks, and Minor Tick Marks **Ⓑ**.

3. If you turn on labels, tap Label Angle to set whether labels run vertically, horizontally, or diagonally **Ⓒ**.

4. Tap anywhere to exit the panel.

To format Y-axis numbers:

1. Tap the chart you want to change. Tap **ⓘ** in the toolbar, and then tap the Y Axis tab.

2. In the Y Axis tab, tap Number Format **Ⓓ**.

3. Choose among the six formatting options **Ⓔ**.

4. Tap anywhere to exit the panel.

Ⓓ In the Y Axis tab, tap Number Format.

Ⓔ Choose among the formatting options.

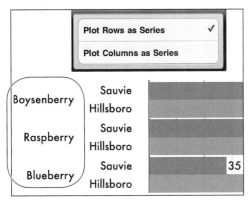

Plotting Series

In charts with data sets from multiple sources, you can control what data is emphasized. To do this, you can plot the rows or columns as a series.

To set how series are plotted:

1. Double-tap the chart to reveal the Edit Data View.

2. Tap ⚙ in the toolbar. From the popover, choose an option based on which data you want to emphasize Ⓐ.

3. Tap done to close the Edit Data View. Depending on your choice, the chart plots the rows as a series Ⓑ or the columns as a series Ⓒ.

Ⓐ In the Edit Data View, tap ⚙ in the toolbar, and choose an option from the popover.

Ⓑ The data is plotted with the *rows* as a series.

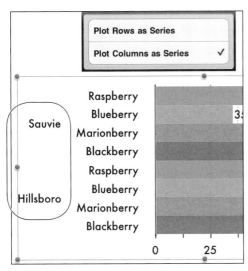

Ⓒ The data is plotted with the *columns* as a series.

Putting It All Together

1. Add several different types of charts to a document.

2. Add a column to a chart, then delete it.

3. Change the color scheme for one of your charts.

4. Change one of your charts to another *type*.

5. Add a title to a chart, then add a legend, positioning the legend so it does not conflict with the title.

6. Change the *size* of your title and legend text.

7. Change the *font* of your title and legend text.

8. Adjust the orientation of your chart's value labels.

9. Use the X Axis and Y Axis tabs to control which items are visible.

9

Working with Tables

Pages for iPad doesn't offer a huge variety of table designs. However, the combinations it does include provide enough options for most users. Table titles, legends, labels, numbers—and their related font and size options—can all be customized with a few taps. You can move, resize, stack, and arrange tables like all other objects in Pages for iPad (see "Arranging Objects and Text" on page 89).

In This Chapter

Adding and Removing Tables

Tables are a great way to visually organize information so that readers can quickly find what they need. Adding a table is easy, as is customizing its look.

To add a table:

1. Tap on the page in the general area where you want to add a table.
2. Tap 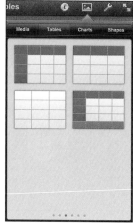 and tap the Tables tab **A**.
3. Swipe through the six panels of color variations for four types of tables. When you find one that suits your needs, tap it, and drag it onto the page.
4. To reposition the table, tap ◎ and drag the table **B**.
5. To resize the table, tap to select it and drag any of the selection handles **C**. After enlarging or shrinking the table, lift your finger off the screen.
6. To add data to a cell, double-tap it and begin typing **D**.

TIP You also can paste content into a cell that you've copied from another page or document.

TIP There's no shortcut to jump from cell to cell. Instead, you have to tap each cell before typing in it.

TIP You cannot insert images in tables.

A Tap and tap the Table tab to choose among four types of tables.

B To reposition the table, tap ◎ and drag the table.

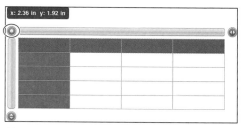

C To resize the table, tap to select it and drag any of the selection handles.

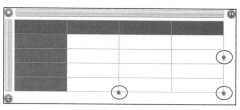

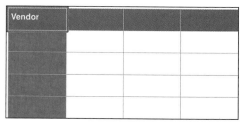

D To enter data into a cell, double-tap it and begin typing.

E To remove a table, tap it, wait a moment, and tap it again. When the pop-up bar appears, tap Delete.

To remove a table:

1. Tap once along the top edge of the table to select it, wait a moment, and then tap once more.

2. When the pop-up bar appears, tap Delete **E**. The table is removed from the page.

TIP If you accidentally select a cell instead of the entire table, just tap well outside the table to start over.

Selecting Cells, Columns, or Rows

With the iPad's touch screen, selecting cells, columns, and rows is a tap-and-drag affair. It's one example where it's easier than using a Mac with a keyboard.

To select a cell:

- Tap the table, then tap the cell you want to select. A blue line appears around its edge Ⓐ. You can now drag the cell elsewhere in the table.

To select multiple cells:

1. Tap the table, then tap the cell you want to select. A blue line appears around its edge Ⓐ.

2. Tap and drag one of the blue selection handles to expand the range of cells selected Ⓑ. You can do this to select an entire row or column Ⓒ.

Product	Stall	Days
Produce	R-5A	M,W,F
Dairy	TBA	TBA
Honey	R-I	Tu, Th

Ⓐ Tap the table, then tap the cell you want to select.

Stall	Days	C
R-5A	M,W,F	7
TBA	TBA	T
R-I	Tu, Th	9
R-7	Sat., Sun.	I
R-16	M,W,F	7

Ⓑ Tap and drag one of the blue selection handles to expand the range of cells selected.

Stall	Days
R-5A	M,W,F
TBA	TBA
R-I	Tu, Th
R-7	Sat., Sun.
R-16	M,W,F
R-4	Sat.,Sun.

Ⓒ You can use the selection handles to select an entire column or row.

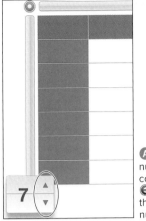

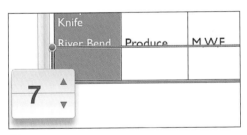

A Change the number of rows or columns by tapping ⊖ or ⊕ and flicking the "flip chart" number.

B Tap Delete in the pop-up bar to delete the *content* in the selected column or row.

C Flick the column or row's "flip chart" to decrease the number.

D The column or row itself is deleted.

Adding or Deleting Columns and Rows

Pages for iPad includes two built-in "flip charts" for changing the number of columns or rows in a table. You cannot use them, however, to delete columns or rows containing data. In those cases, you need to first select and delete the data.

To add or remove columns and rows:

1. Tap to select the table.

2. Tap ⊖ or ⊕ and flick the "flip chart" to increase or decrease the display number **A**.

3. When you're done, tap anywhere on the screen outside the table.

> **TIP** It's easy to accidentally close the counter by tapping it. Instead, try a gentle up or down flick—as if you were flipping numbers on a wheel.

To delete columns or rows with data:

1. Tap the table, then select the column or row you want to delete.

2. Wait a moment after the blue selection handles appear, then tap the column or row.

3. Tap Delete in the pop-up bar **B**. The *content* in the column or row is deleted, but the column or row itself remains.

4. With the column or row still selected, you can flick its "flip chart" to decrease the number **C**. The column or row itself is deleted **D**.

Moving Cell Content

Moving content from one cell to another is an example of how Pages for iPad takes advantage of the iPad. Using this approach, you can reshuffle the content of a table more quickly than possible with a keyboard.

To move content from one cell to another:

1. Tap the table, then tap the cell whose content you want to move. A blue line appears around its edge.

2. Place your finger on the highlighted cell—don't tap, just touch. Drag your finger and the cell content moves with it 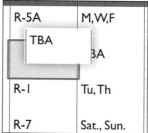.

3. Keep dragging your finger to another cell, which becomes highlighted 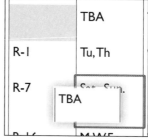.

4. Lift your finger and the content of the first cell replaces the content of the second 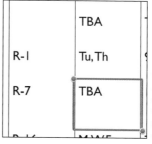. The first cell is now blank.

> **TIP** You cannot move header cell content to a regular table cell. However, you can move the content of a regular cell to a header cell. (See "Changing Table Layout" later in this chapter for more on headers.)

A Touch your finger to a selected cell, then drag it to move the cell content.

B When your finger passes over another cell, it's highlighted.

C Lift your finger and the content of the first cell replaces the second. The first cell is now blank.

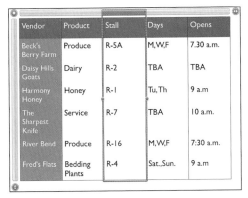

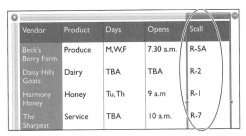

A Tap and hold the bar above the column or row until it turns blue.

B Drag the column or row to another spot in the table.

C Lift your finger and the column or row snaps to its new location.

Moving and Resizing Columns or Rows

It's almost as easy to move a column or row as it is to move a cell. You also can quickly widen or narrow columns and rows as needed.

To move a column or row:

1. Tap the table, then tap and hold your finger on the part of the top or right bar that corresponds to the column or row you want to move A.

2. When that part of the bar turns blue, drag the column or row to another place in the table B.

3. Lift your finger from the screen and the column or row snaps to its new location in the table C.

To resize a column or row:

1. Tap the table, then tap and hold your finger on the part of the top or right bar that corresponds to the column or row you want to resize.

2. When that part of the bar turns blue, tap the small double bar **D**.

3. Drag the double bar in either direction to resize the selected column or row **E**.

4. When you're finished, lift your finger and tap anywhere on the screen to deselect the column or row.

D Tap and hold the bar above the column or row until it turns blue, then tap the small double bar.

E Drag the double bar in either direction to resize the column or row.

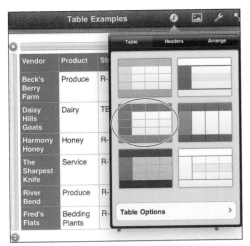

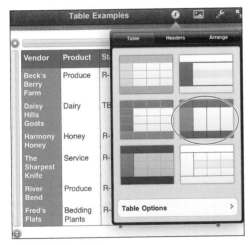

Changing Table Colors

You can change the colors of a table at any time, so you're never locked into a particular look.

To change table colors:

1. Tap the table, tap **ⓘ** in the toolbar, and then tap the Table tab **Ⓐ**.

2. Tap one of the six color schemes to apply it to the table **Ⓑ**. Close the tab by tapping anywhere on the screen.

Ⓐ To change a selected table's colors, tap **ⓘ** in the toolbar, and tap the Table tab.

Ⓑ Tap one of the six color schemes to apply it to the table.

Changing Table Layout

Beyond changing the colors for a table, you also can set how many header and footer rows are displayed; whether to alternate row colors to help readers scan wide lines; plus change the table's text size and font. Header and footer rows are useful for adding extra labeling or explanation to tables.

To set header and footer options:

1. Tap the table to select it, tap **ⓘ** in the toolbar, and then tap the Headers tab **Ⓐ**.

2. Lightly flick the arrows on the "flip charts" to change the number of header rows, header columns, or footer rows used in the table **Ⓑ**.

3. Tap anywhere to close the tab.

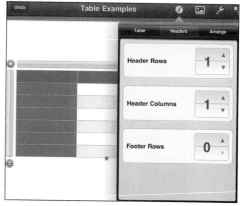

Ⓐ Tap the table to select it, tap **ⓘ** in the toolbar, and then tap the Headers tab.

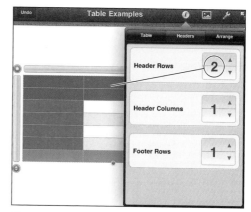

Ⓑ Tap the arrows on the "flip charts" to change how many header rows, header columns, or footer rows are applied.

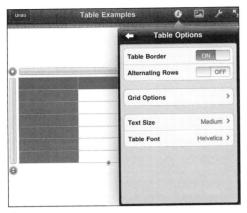

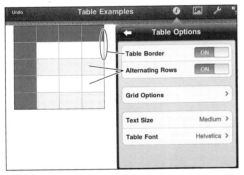

C In the Table Options panel, tap Table Border or Alternating Rows to turn either option on or off.

D The table reflects your choices. Here Table Border and Alternating Rows have been applied.

E In the Table Options panel, tap Text Size.

To turn on the table border or alternating rows:

1. Tap the table you want to change. Tap **i** in the toolbar, tap the Table tab, and then tap Table Options.

2. In the Table Options panel, tap Table Border or Alternating Rows to turn either option on or off C. The table reflects your choices D.

3. When you're satisfied with your choices, tap ◄ to return to the Table tab or tap anywhere on the screen to close the panel.

TIP There is no option for creating alternating column colors.

To change text size:

1. Tap the table you want to change. Tap **i** in the toolbar, tap the Table tab, and then tap Table Options.

2. In the Table Options panel, tap Text Size E.

3. Tap another text size and the table's text immediately changes F. When you're satisfied with your choice, tap ◄ to return to the Table Options panel or tap anywhere on the screen to close the panel.

F Tap another text size and the table's text immediately changes.

To change the table's font:

1. Tap the table you want to change. Tap
   ⓘ in the toolbar, tap the Table tab, and
   then tap Table Options.

2. In the Table Options panel, tap Table
   Font **ⓖ**.

3. Scroll through the font family listings
   until you find one you like. If a font family includes several typefaces, there's
   a blue arrow on the right **ⓗ**. Tap the
   arrow to choose among the typefaces.

4. Tap a typeface to apply it **ⓘ**. Tap **⬅** to
   return to the Table Options panel or tap
   anywhere on the screen to close the
   panel.

ⓖ In the Table Options panel, tap
Table Font.

ⓗ If a font family includes several typefaces,
there's a blue arrow on the right.

ⓘ Tap a typeface to apply it.

A In the Table Options panel, tap Grid Options.

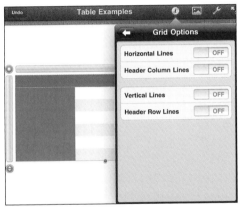

B The table with all the Grid Options turned off.

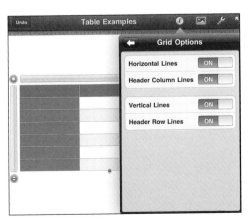

C The table with all four Grid Options turned on.

Setting Grid Options

You have control over how Pages for iPad formats grids within tables. You can display horizontal lines, vertical lines, and lines in headers—or you can turn off the lines entirely. Showing gridlines often makes tables easier to read.

To set grid options:

1. Tap the table, tap ⓘ in the toolbar, and then tap the Table tab.

2. In the Table Options panel, tap Grid Options A.

3. Choose among the four options for turning on or off Horizontal Lines, Header Column Lines, Vertical Lines, and Header Row Lines B, C.

4. Tap ◀ to return to the Table Options panel or tap anywhere on the screen to close the panel.

Putting It All Together

1. Add a table of any type to a document. Add data to the table.

2. Add another table to the document and then delete it.

3. Add some empty columns and rows to your first table. Remove an empty column or row.

4. Delete a column or row that contains data.

5. Practice selecting a single cell and then multiple cells.

6. Move content from one cell to another.

7. Move and resize several columns and rows.

8. Change the table colors.

9. Change the table's footer, format it for alternating row colors, and change the text size or font.

Index

Import Document dialog, 39
importing
    documents emailed to iPad, 43
    documents using iTunes, 38–40
    images, 74–75
insertion point
    inserting text at, 21
    using magnifying glass at, 19, 22
iPad
    emailing files to/from, 42–43
    external keyboard for, 14–15
    importing documents emailed to, 43
    navigation screens for, 10
    photo imports using Camera Connector, 75
    screen keyboard for, 12–13, 22
    selecting text from, 19–20
    syncing images from iTunes to, 74
iPhoto, 74
iTunes
    exporting iPad documents via, 36–37
    importing documents to iPad via, 38–40
    syncing images to iPad with, 74
iWork.com, 44

K

keyboard dock, 14
keyboards
    external, 14–15
    letters, 64
    navigating between tab stops on, 64
    using iPad's screen, 12–13, 14, 22

L

Label Angle panel, 111
launching Pages for iPad, 24
layout for columns, 65
legends, 107, 108
letters keyboard, 12, 13
lists, 59–60

M

magnifying glass icon, 19, 22
margin markers, 61, 62
margins
    page, 30–31
    setting paragraph, 61–62
masking images, 81
matching size of objects, 93
Media tab (Document Setup view), 83
Microsoft Word
    compatibility with Pages for iPad, 40, 41
    file format for, 36
    printing iPad documents with, 48

moving
    cell content, 120
    chart legends, 107
    objects, 79
    objects with text, 99
    table columns and rows, 121–122
multi-finger swipe, 90–91
multiple screens, 10
My Documents button, 24

N

narrowing text selection, 20
navigating
    cell to cell, 116
    jumping to top of document, 18
    Pages for iPad documents, 17–18
    between tab stops, 64
New Documents button, 24, 26
nudging objects, 90–91
numbers
    formatting on axis, 112
    page, 33, 34

O

objects
    deleting, 94
    matching size of, 93
    moving in Pages, 79
    moving with text, 99
    nudging, 90–91
    resizing, 80
    rotating, 11
    selecting multiple, 91, 92
    spacing between text and, 99
    stacking, 96–97
    working with edge guides, 91, 95
    wrapping text around, 98–99
Open In popover, 43
opening
    iPad documents in Pages for Mac, 37
    items in iPad, 10
    Pages for iPad, 16
orientation
    keyboard's alignment to current, 12
    viewing full pages in Portrait, 30

P

page breaks, 65, 68
pages (document)
    margins, 30
    numbering, 33
    size of, 31